AN ANALYTICAL APPROACH TO

MIND-BODY CONNECTION

AND

CREATIVE PHRASING

Lang Zhao

Violet Anamnesis Publications
STUDIO CITY, CALIFORNIA

Copyright © 2019 by **Violet Anamnesis Publications**

All rights reserved. No part of this publication may be reproduced, distributed or transmitted in any form or by any means, including photocopying, recording, or other electronic or mechanical methods, without prior written permission from the publisher, except in the case of brief quotations embodied in critical reviews and certain other noncommercial uses permitted by copyright law. For permission requests, write to the publisher, addressed "Attention: Permissions Coordinator," at the address below.

Violet Anamnesis Publications
4112 Whitsett Ave, Suite 204
Studio City, CA 91604
www.violetanamnesispublications.com

Contributor **David Myers Jr.**
Co-researched on the CPS part by **David Myers Jr.**
Assistant & Coordinator **Ziyin Zhao**
Proofread by **Ziyin Zhao, David Myers Jr.**
Author Photo by **Ekaterina Gorbacheva**
Cover artwork by **Nyla McDaniel**

An Analytical Approach to Mind-Body Connection and Creative Phrasing/Lang Zhao -- 1st ed.
ISBN 978-1-944213-90-9

Table of Contents

Introduction i

Part 1 Mind: Expanding your sonic vocabulary 1

  Session 1: Hearing the upbeats 2

  Session 2: Getting familiar with odd groupings—3-note groupings 9
    2.1: 16th note subdivision 3-note groupings 9
    2.2: Setting up figures using 16th note subdivision 3-note groupings 10
    2.3: Metric modulation 14
    2.4: 3-note groupings and 4-limb interdependence 16

  Session 3: Getting familiar with odd groupings—5-note groupings 18
    3.1: 16th note subdivision 5-note groupings 18
    3.2: Setting up figures using 16th note subdivision 5-note groupings 19
    3.3: Eighth note triplet subdivision 5-note groupings 21
    3.4: Setting up figures using 8th note triplet subdivision 5-note groupings 22
    3.5: Eighth note triplet subdivision 5-note groupings in 15/16 24
    3.6: 5-note groupings and 4-limb interdependence 25

  Session 4: Getting familiar with odd groupings—7-note groupings 27
    4.1: 16th note subdivision 7-note groupings 27
    4.2: Setting up figures using 16th note subdivision 7-note groupings 28
    4.3: 8th note triplet subdivision 7-note groupings 30
    4.4: Setting up figures using 8th note triplet subdivision 7-note groupings 31
    4.5: 7-note groupings and 4-limb interdependence 33

Session 5: Integrating odd groupings and upbeats phrasing into grooves and chops 34
    5.1: From sonic vocabulary to sticking vocabulary 35
    5.2: From sonic vocabulary to groove constructions 40
        (a): Bass drum note placement 40
        (b): Ghost note control 41

Part 2 – Body: Enhancing your mobility and balance 43

Session 6: Enhancing your mobility 44
    6.1: Single directional paths with single stroke roll 45
    6.2: Changing directions by adding an odd number of strokes 46
    6.3: Changing directions by adding diddles 49
    6.4: Diagnostic paths 52
    6.5: Irregular stickings 54

Session 7: Enhancing your balance 56
    7.1: Balancing yourself and your drum set 56
    7.2: Balancing your weak side 57
    7.3: Balancing your hands and feet 64
    7.4: Advancing your balance 68

Part 3 – Mind-body connection: the Creative Phrasing System (CPS) 71

Session 8: Exploring spaces 72
    8.1: At the micro level—exploring spaces at different rates 72
    8.2: At the macro level—exploring the full phrase in different ways 76
        (a): Stretch and compression of time 76
        (b): Relative position of figures 78

Session 9: Creative sticking part 1—sticking sound texture ... 81
9.1: Sound texture of double stroke roll variations ... 81
(a): Inverted double stroke roll ... 81
(b): Short roll variations with similar sonic vocabulary ... 84
9.2: Sound texture of paradiddle family stickings ... 86
9.3: Sound texture of flams ... 91
(a): Flam variations ... 91
(b): Flam orchestrations ... 93

Session 10: Creative sticking part 2—sticking morphing ... 95
10.1: Morphing from flams ... 95
10.2: Morphing into flams ... 97
10.3: Comprehensive morphing ... 100

Session 11: Displacement and metric modulation ... 103
11.1: Permutation ... 103
11.2: Phrase displacement/short turn-around patterns ... 106
11.3: Metric modulation ... 107

Session 12: Real world example analysis ... 108
12.1: Drum solo excerpt 1 analysis—The Resonance Project "Neo Thangka" ... 109
12.2: Drum solo excerpt 2 analysis—The Resonance Project "A Progression to Infinity" .. 112

Conclusion ... 115

About the Author ... 117

Introduction

Teaching one to fish is better than giving one the fish.

In my last book, *"An Analytical Approach to Linear Applications: Integrating Gospel Drumming into Your Grooves and Chops"*, the analytical approach was introduced to help you to understand the key characteristics of gospel drumming, such as tone, touch, feel, etc. We also looked into linear drumming and took inspiration from how gospel musicians think. Finally, I introduced the concept of sonic vocabulary and mind-body connection, and demonstrated how they relate to phrasing using linear drumming.

Let's pick up where we have left from the last book and look deeper into mind-body connection and creative phrasing. You will find more advanced materials focusing on improving your mind, body, mind-body connection, and creative phrasing. The concepts and examples in this book are widely used in gospel drumming and many other drumming styles such as jazz, fusion, rock, metal, etc. I hope the content will help you to develop your very own unique playing and voice while going through this book.

We are going to discuss about how to train your mind and body separately first, then focus more on mind-body connection and creative phrasing in the following order:

Part 1. Mind: Expanding your sonic vocabulary

Part 2. Body: Enhancing your mobility and balance

Part 3. Mind-body connection: The Creative Phrasing System (CPS)

Please visit *http://www.langzhaomusic.com/book-a2* **for video materials.**

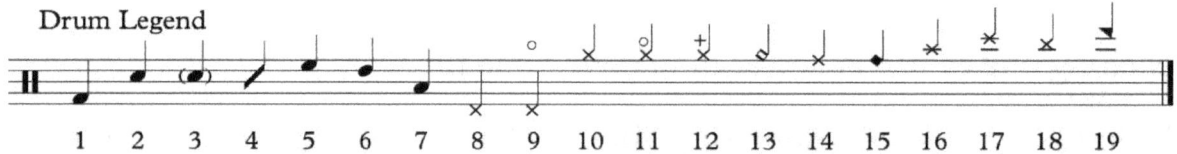

1. Kick	8. Hi-hat foot stroke	15. Ride bell
2. Snare	9. Hi-hat foot splash	16. Low crash
3. Snare ghost note	10. Hi-hat	17. High crash
4. Snare rim shot	11. Start to open Hi-Hats	18. Splash
5. High tom	12. Close the Hi-Hats	19. Stack
6. Mid tom	13. Open Hi-hat	
7. Low tom	14. Ride	

Part 1
Mind:

Expanding your sonic vocabulary

Improving your mind should always be the priority during the training process. Great music ideas always come from great minds. In this part you will learn how to expand your sonic vocabulary by improving your ability to hear the upbeats and odd groupings. Mastering these elements will bring your phrasing to a new dimension.

Session 1: Hearing the upbeats

Subdividing a quarter note pulse into 16th note or 8th note triplet subdivisions, is probably two of the most common things we as drummers do daily. They are fundamental, but very critical. Let's look at everything under a 4/4 context for now:

Example 1:

When a quarter note pulse is subdivided as shown in example 1, it is very natural for us to feel and gravitate our hearing to the downbeat "1", "2", "3", "4" or to the 8th note upbeat "+". Once we have them clearly marked out, it is easy to fill in the rest of the subdivisions. The ability to hear the 16th note and 8th note triplet upbeats independently will give you many more possibilities, color, and add richness to your phrasing. Note that these 16th upbeats are "e"s and "a"s in 16th note subdivisions, and 8th note triplet upbeats are "+"s and "a"s in 8th note triplet subdivisions.

The goal in this session is to improve your sense of these upbeats, so that you can hear them more independently without relying on the downbeat too much. This will not only help you to expand your sonic vocabulary to assist further exploration of creative phrasing, but also improve your sense of timing accuracy and consistency.

In my first book, a whole session was dedicated to how to use metronome creatively. Let's review it and use the following three metronome systems to go over each exercise below. Please also *make sure to keep a pulse with your hi-hat foot. It could be either a quarter note pulse, an 8th note upbeat pulse, or 2 and 4 pulses.*

AN ANALYTICAL APPROACH TO MIND-BODY CONNECTION AND CREATIVE PHRASING

Metronome system

1. *Mark out all subdivisions.*
2. *Mark out only "e"s and "a"s for 16th note subdivision exercises and "+"s in 8th note subdivision exercises.*
3. *Mark out the quarter note pulse only.*

Work through the following exercises thoroughly to build a solid foundation for the upcoming sessions.

Exercise 1:

Exercise 2:

Exercise 3:

Exercise 4:

Exercise 5:

Play the rhythms (Exercise 1-4) above on the snare with the following ostinato system:

1. Quarter note pulse on hi-hat and 8th note on ride

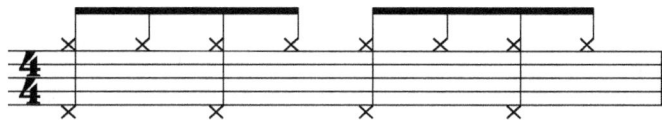

2. Eighth note pulse on hi-hat and ride

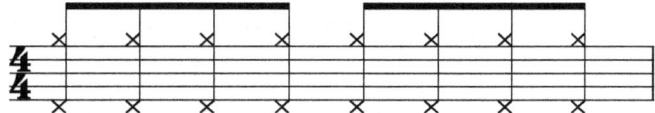

3. Play a regular time jazz ride on 8th note triplet patterns and double time straight jazz over 16th note patterns.

For example, in Exercise 4, if we apply the concepts above, bar 17-20 will become:

Exercise 6:

Play the rhythms (Exercise 1-4) above with the snare and bass drum in unison, as well as the second ostinato pattern above.

Exercise 7:

Keep a quarter note pulse on the Hi-hat using your foot, use the other three limbs to play the rhythms, and improvise using combinations of single voice, two voices (two limbs in unison), and three voices (three limbs in unison).

Again, it is very important to be able to hear the upbeats independently. How fast you can play solidly is determined by how fast you are able to hear the upbeats independently. Such ability can greatly improve your consistency of rate, general timing, and let you start and end a phrase creatively. Starting from the next session, let's go a step further to talk about odd groupings. A solid sense of upbeats is the foundation of further exploration of odd groupings.

Session 2: Getting familiar with odd groupings—3-note groupings

Once you get a good sense of the upbeats, you can move on to the odd groupings. Let's still put things in 4/4 and 16th note subdivisions for now. When applying odd groupings of 16th notes over 4/4 meter, you will naturally start to land your phrases on some of the upbeats. In this session, let's look at the 3-note groupings.

2.1: 16th note subdivision 3-note groupings

Let's look at the first example.

Example 1:

3-note groupings will overlap back to 1 in every three bars, with a very distinct accent pattern of "downbeat, a, +, e". Please go through the following exercises to get familiar with the accent positions and flow. Make sure to set your metronome at a comfortable tempo and mark out all 16th note subdivisions.

Exercise 1:

1. Sing all the 16th note subdivisions and accent the downbeats. Use your hands to clap out the odd grouping accents.

2. Sing all the 16th note subdivisions and accent the odd grouping accents. Use your hands to clap out the quarter note pulse.

3. Sing all the 16th note subdivisions with emphasis on the downbeats and the odd grouping accents. Use your hands to clap out the odd grouping accents.

Keep in mind again that 3-note groupings will overlap back to 1 every three bars, with a very distinct accent pattern of "downbeat, a, +, e".

2.2: Setting up figures using 16th note subdivision 3-note groupings

In the following example, you will be looking at a very common 16th note groove in a 4-bar phrase, and you will set up the figure at "e" of the third beat.

Example 2:

In a more common way, you probably would play a fill leading to the downbeat "3" before the figure:

Example 3:

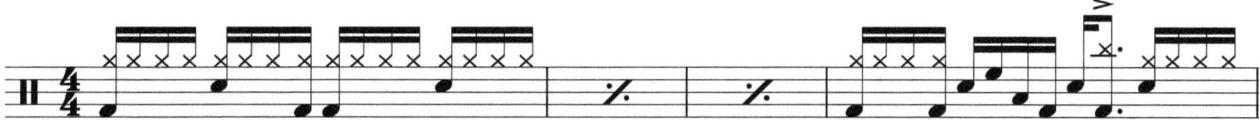

The next example shows setting up the figure using 3-note groupings starting on:

1. "1" of bar 4
2. "1a" of bar 4
3. "4e" of bar 3

Example 4:

Please work on the exercise from the next page. Play any 16th note-based groove and use 3-note groupings to work on the set-up phrases for the figures. Try to start from different spots of the 3-note grouping reference below.

Reference

Exercise 2: setting up figures with 3-note groupings

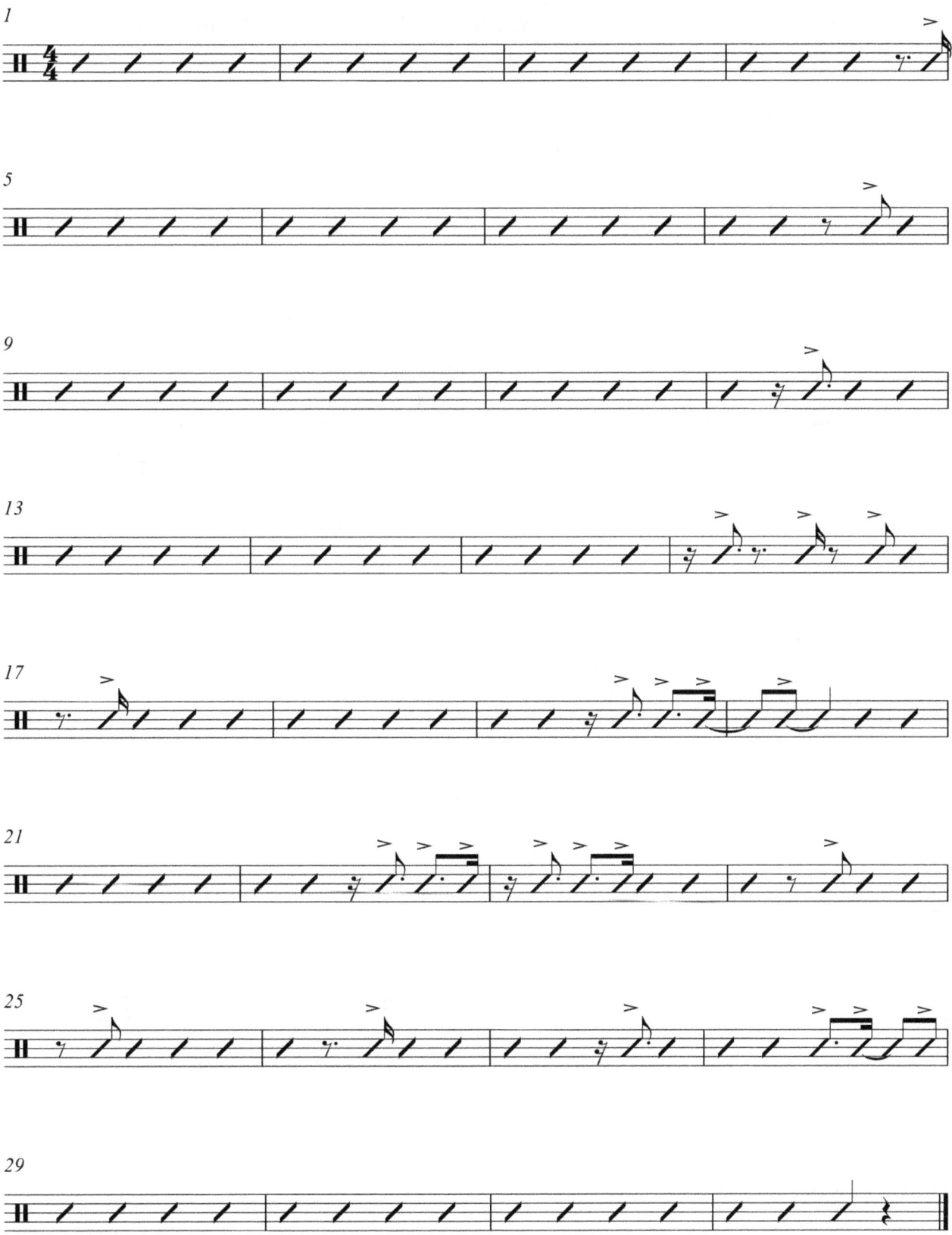

2.3: Metric modulation

Again, under a 4/4 with 16th note subdivision context, you can easily tell two things from the example below:

1. Every four cycles of 3-note groupings will align with every three cycles of 4-note groupings.

2. Each cycle of 3-note groupings will align with each cycle of 3-quarter note pulses.

Example 5:

Since the value of a 16th note subdivision 3-note grouping is equal to a dotted 8th note, you are now superimposing dotted 8th note pulses on top of the original quarter note pulses. Please see the example below.

Example 6:

Now if you put every 4 dotted 8th note groupings into a new bar, you will get a new 4-bar phrase of 4/4 by treating the dotted eighth notes as new quarter note pulses. See the example below.

Example 7:

If you look at the new 4-bar phrase and the original 3-bar phrase, they should have the same length, which means the total value of the new 16 quarter notes in the 4-bar phrase should be equal to the original 12 quarter notes in the 3-bar phrase. But in order to make them equal, you will have to apply a new tempo to the new 4-bar phrase. Let's say if the old tempo was quarter note = 90bpm, then the new tempo should be quarter note = 120bpm. Please see the example below:

Example 8:

How to calculate this?

From Example 5, you know that each cycle of 3-note groupings will align with each cycle of 3 quarter note pulses.

In Example 7, you come up with the new 4-bar phrase by realizing each dotted 8th note pulse (value of one 3-note grouping) as a new quarter note pulse.

So, in the new 4-bar phrase, the total value of *every 4 quarter* notes equals to the total value of the old 3-bar phrase's *every 3 quarter notes*. We will call them the pivot note value.

New tempo/Old tempo= New pivot value/Old pivot value

In this case, the new tempo's calculation would be:

New tempo/90bpm=4/3

New tempo=120bpm

2.4: 3-note groupings and 4-limb interdependence

The following exercise is designed to help you develop 4-limb interdependence. This will eventually become something very useful for phrasing within a groove. Play the ostinato and use your other two limbs to play each pattern under the ostinato. Make sure to count out loud and use metronome to regulate your note placements.

Exercise 3:

Ostinato: Ride cymbal and foot- controlled open/close hi-hat

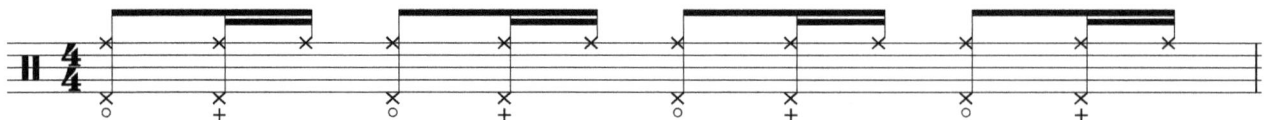

3-note grouping patterns

Session 3: Getting familiar with odd groupings—5-note groupings

Now let's move on to 5-note groupings, which are very commonly used nowadays just like 3-note groupings. They have very distinguished sound characteristics that create more tension in a phrase than 3-note groupings do. Let's follow the same steps by first looking at the exact landing point of each grouping.

3.1: 16th note subdivision 5-note groupings

Example 1:

Let's put this in 4/4 again. 5-note groupings will resolve back to 1 every five bars, with a very distinct accent pattern of "downbeat, e, +, a". In order to get familiar with the accent flow and position, please go through the following exercises. Make sure to set your metronome at a comfortable tempo and mark out all 16th note subdivisions.

Exercise 1:

1. Sing all the 16th note subdivisions and accent the downbeats. Use your hands to clap out the odd grouping accents.

2. Sing all the 16th note subdivisions and accent the odd grouping accents. Use your hands to clap out the quarter note pulse.

3. Sing all the 16th note subdivisions with emphasis on the downbeats and the odd grouping accents. Use your hands to clap out the odd grouping accents.

3.2: Setting up figures using 16th note subdivision 5-note groupings

In the next example, you will be looking at a very common 16th note groove in a 4-bar phrase, with a figure at "e" of the third beat. In the examples, 5-note groupings are used to set up the figures starting from different spots. Work on setting up figures using 5-note groupings with exercise 2.

Example 2:

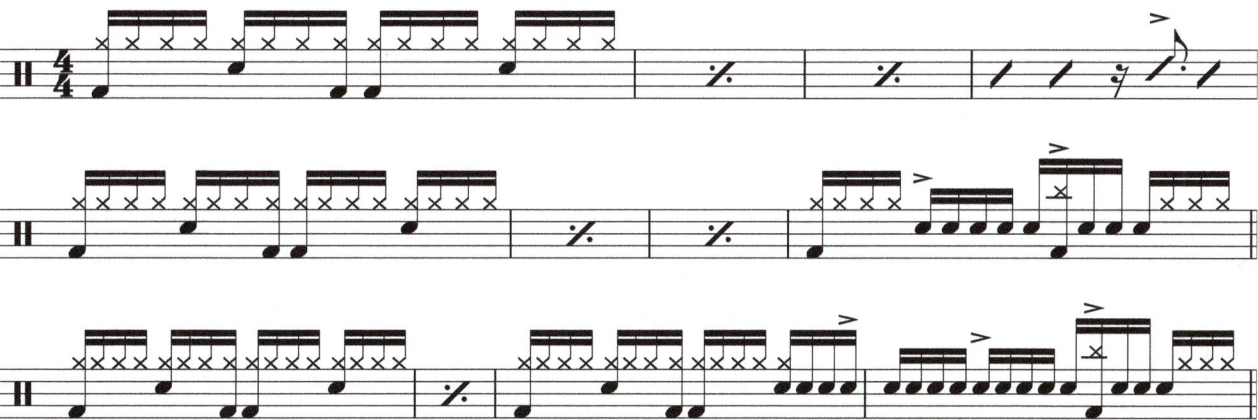

Exercise 2: Setting up figures with 16th note subdivision 5-note groupings

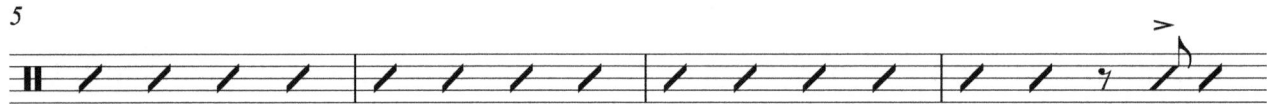

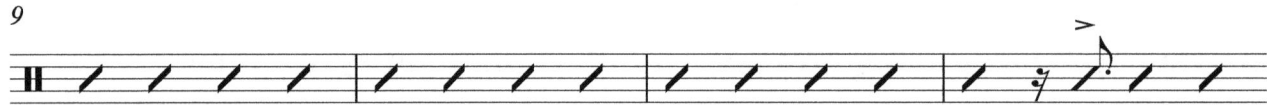

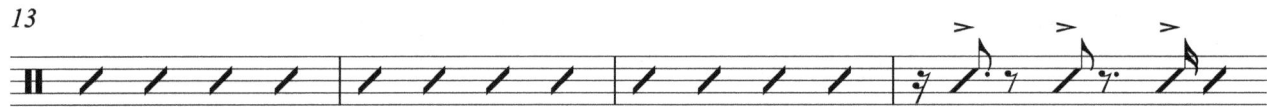

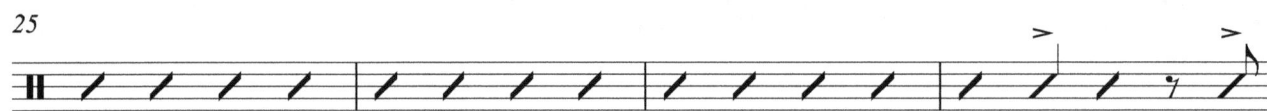

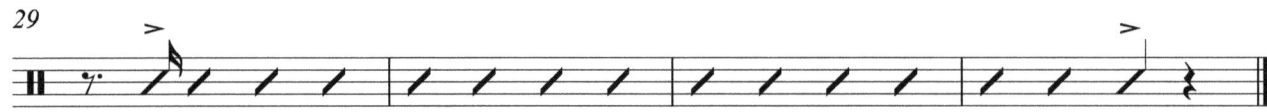

3.3: Eighth note triplet subdivision 5-note groupings

Now let's superimpose 5-note groupings over 3-note groupings. This is commonly found in jazz applications, where you are putting 8th note triplet 5-note groupings over the quarter note pulse.

Example 3:

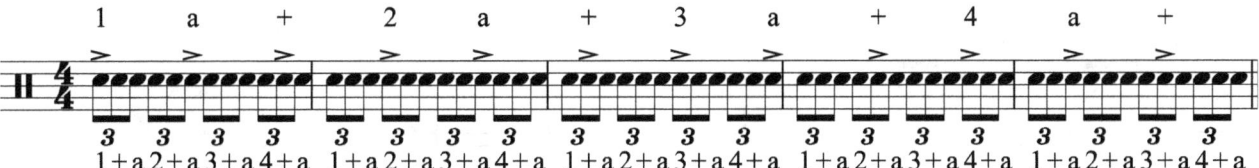

The 5-note groupings now follow a very clear accent pattern "1, a, +" against the 8th note triplet subdivision.

Exercise 3:

1. Sing all the 8th note triplet subdivisions and accent the downbeats. Use your hands to clap out the odd grouping accents.

2. Sing all the 8th note triplet subdivisions and accent the odd grouping accents. Use your hands to clap out the quarter note pulse.

3. Sing all the 8th note triplet subdivisions with emphasis on the downbeats and the odd grouping accents. Use your hands to clap out the odd grouping accents.

3.4: Setting up figures using 8th note triplet subdivision 5-note groupings

The next example is a very common jazz groove in a 4-bar phrase, with a figure at "a" of the third beat for you to set up. Work on setting up figures using 5-note groupings with exercise 4.

Example 4:

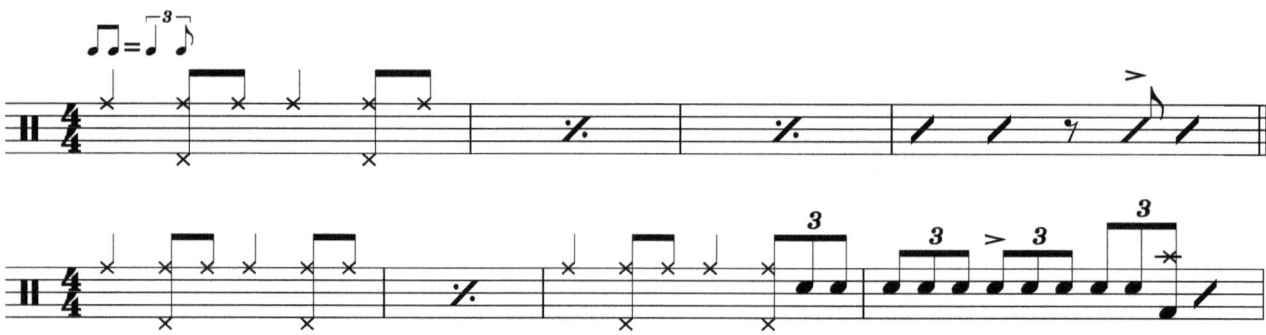

Exercise 4: Setting up figures with 8th note triplet subdivision 5-note groupings

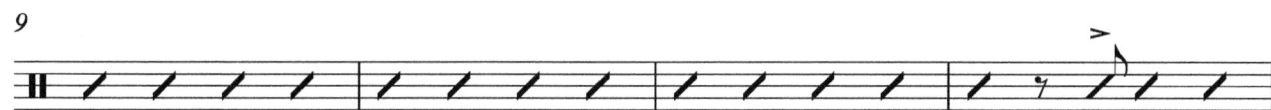

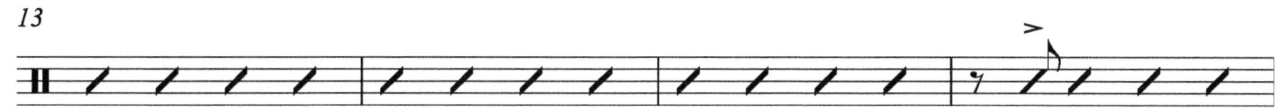

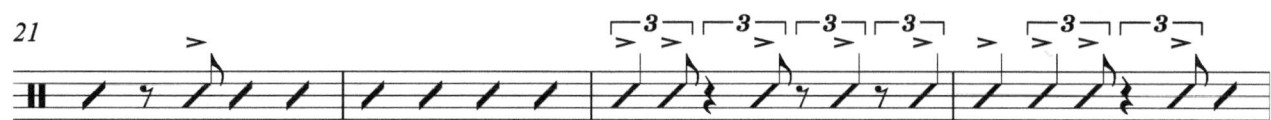

3.5: Eighth note triplet subdivision 5-note groupings in 15/16

15/16 is a very interesting meter in which you can group 16th notes into either 3-note groupings or 5-note groupings. When playing them simultaneously by superimposing one on top of each other, you will hear this very melodic and syncopated pattern.

Example 5:

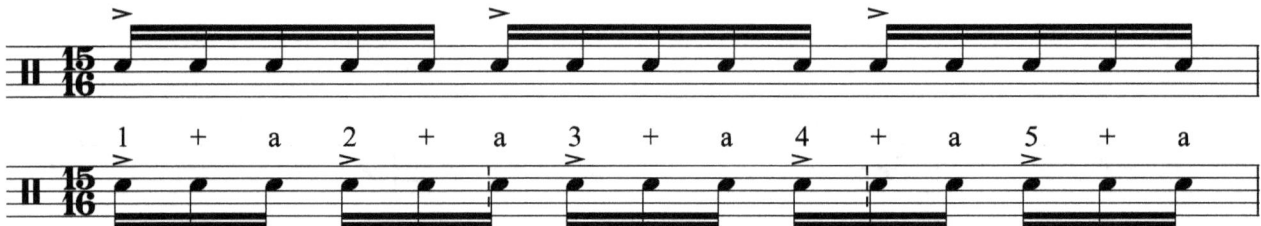

Since 3 and 5 are common divisors of 15, it takes only one bar of 15/16 for three 5-note groupings and five 3-note groupings to line up. Grouping 15/16 in either way will provide you some sort of a feel of three. When we divide it into three 5-note groupings, it has a big "3" feel; it's kind of like 3/4 when playing quintuplet subdivisions. When dividing 15/16 into five 3-note groupings, you have these smaller "3" feel, which is kind of like subdividing the 8th note pulses in 5/8 with triplet.

When layering both groupings, you will get this very syncopated pattern:

$$1 \cdot \cdot \; 2 \cdot a \; 3 \cdot \cdot \; 4 + \cdot \; 5 \cdot \cdot$$

In the next exercise, you will get familiar with both accent patterns by working on switching from one to another. Use metronome to mark out all subdivisions to ensure your note-placements are correct. It is very important to know exactly where each accent falls at. Notice the third and fourth lines are the same sonically; but if you think in different groupings, they are actually different.

Exercise 5:

The next step is to move to the drum set and orchestrate each accent pattern into grooves. No examples are provided here. Please use your creativity and play/write/work out a groove.

3.6: 5-note groupings and 4-limb interdependence

The following exercise is designed to help you develop your 4-limb interdependence. As I mentioned in the previous session, interdependence is very useful for phrasing within a groove. Play the ostinato and use your other two limbs to play each pattern under the ostinato. Make sure to count out loud and use a metronome to regulate your note placements.

Exercise 6:

Ostinato 1: Ride cymbal and foot-controlled open/close hi-hat

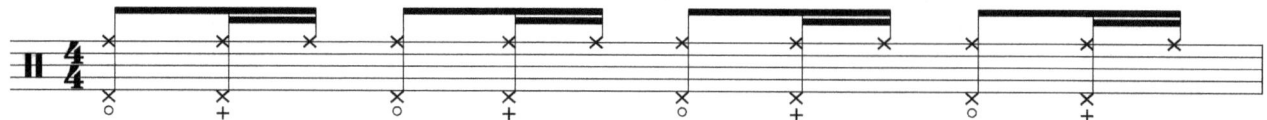

Ostinato 2: Jazz ride and hi-hat patterns

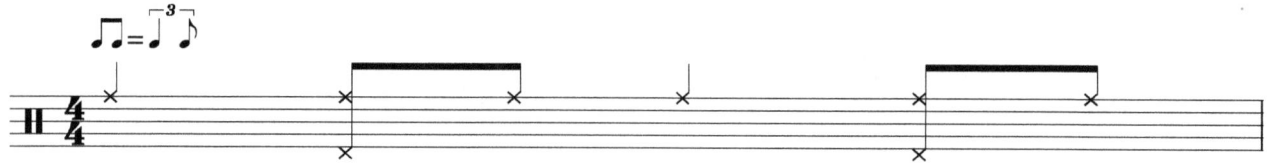

5-note grouping patterns (treat them as 8th notes when working on Ostinato 2)

Session 4: Getting familiar with odd groupings—7-note groupings

Now let's move on to 7-note groupings. 3-note groupings and 5-note groupings have a shorter turn-around. When you get to 7-note groupings, those couple of extra notes make them sound less intense but add more tension to your phrasing at the same time.

4.1: 16th note subdivision 7-note groupings

Example 1:

In 4/4, 7-note groupings will resolve back to 1 in every seven bars, with a very distinct accent pattern of "downbeat, a, +, e". The following exercise will help you to get familiar with the accent pattern's flow. Make sure to set your metronome at a comfortable tempo and mark out all 16th note subdivisions.

Exercise 1:

1. Sing all the 16th note subdivisions and accent the downbeats. Use your hands to clap out the odd grouping accents.

2. Sing all the 16th note subdivisions and accent the odd grouping accents. Use your hands to clap out the quarter note pulse.

3. Sing all the 16th note subdivisions with emphasis on the downbeats and the odd grouping accents. Use your hands to clap out the odd grouping accents.

4.2: Setting up figures using 16th note subdivision 7-note groupings

In the next example, you will be looking at a very common 16th note groove in a 4-bar phrase, with a figure at "e" of the third beat to set up. Work on setting up figures using 7-note groupings with exercise 2.

Example 2:

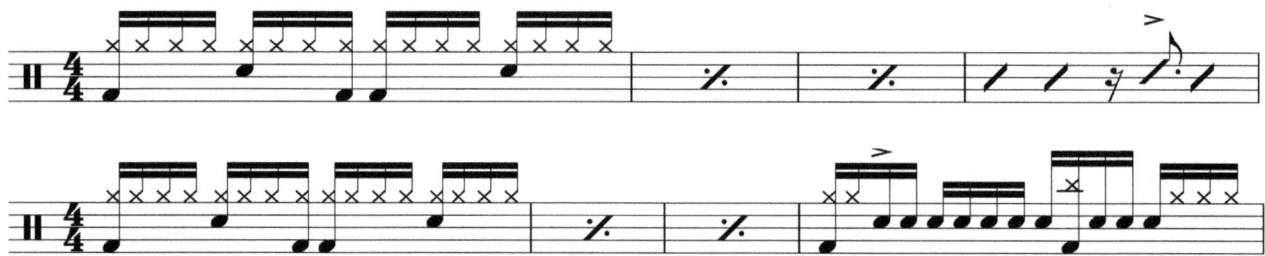

Exercise 2: Setting up figures with 16th note subdivision 7-note groupings

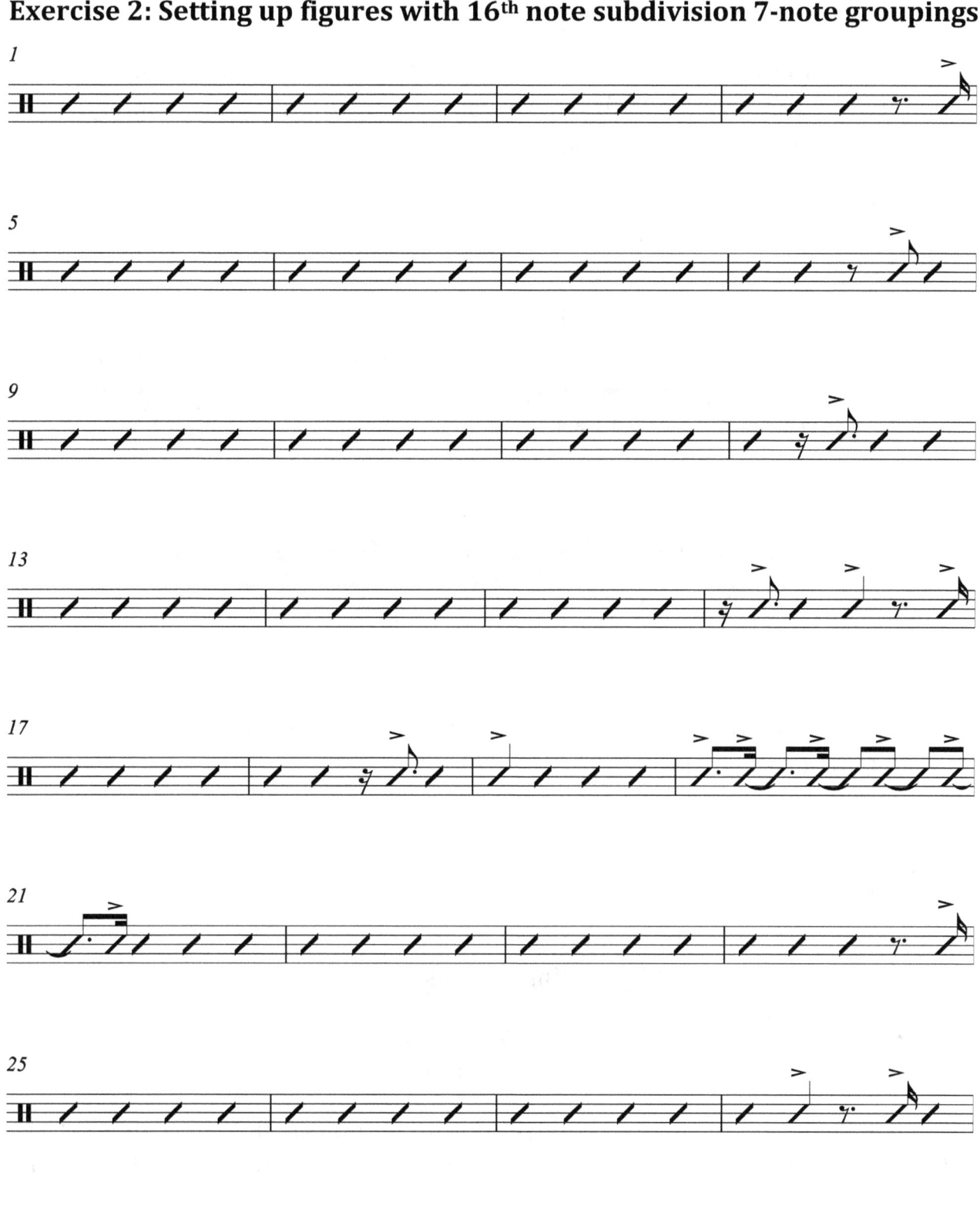

4.3: 8th note triplet subdivision 7-note groupings

Now let's look at how to superimpose 7-note groupings over 3-note groupings. This is commonly used in jazz as well, where you are putting 8th note triplet 7-note groupings over the quarter note pulse.

Example 3:

The 7-note groupings follow a very clear accent pattern of "downbeat, +, a" against the 8th note triplet subdivision.

Exercise 3:

1. Sing all the 8th note triplet subdivisions and accent the downbeats. Use your hands to clap out the odd grouping accents.

2. Sing all the 8th note triplet subdivisions and accent the odd grouping accents. Use your hands to clap out the quarter note pulse.

3. Sing all the 8th note triplet subdivisions with emphasis on the downbeats and the odd grouping accents. Use your hands to clap out the odd grouping accents.

4.4: Setting up figures using 8th note triplet subdivision 7-note groupings

The next example is a very common jazz groove in a 4-bar phrase, with a figure at "a" of the third beat to set up. Work on setting up figures using 7-note groupings with exercise 4.

Example 4:

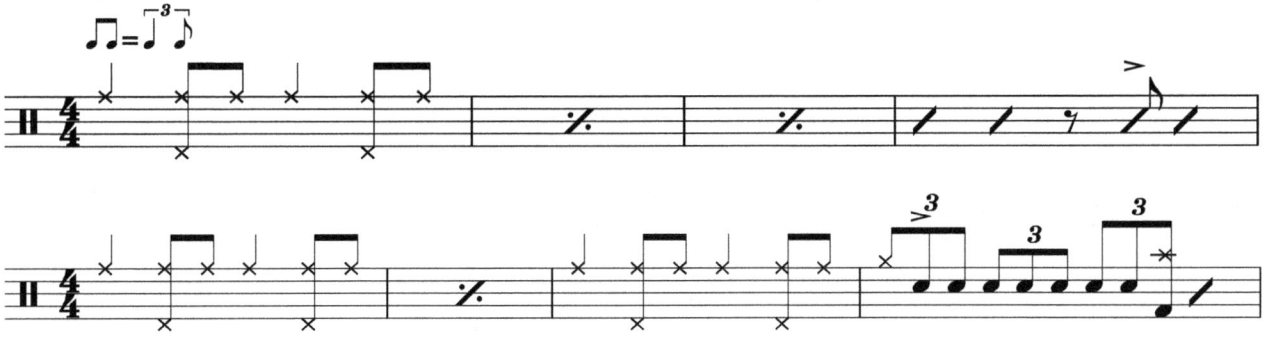

Exercise 4: Setting up figures with 8th note triplet subdivision 7-note groupings

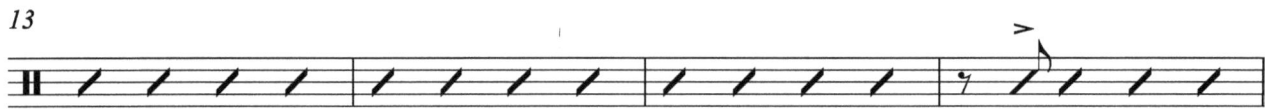

4.5: 7-note groupings and 4-limb interdependence

The following exercise is designed to help you develop 4-limb interdependence. Play the ostinato and use your other two limbs to play each pattern under the ostinato. Make sure to count out loud and use metronome to regulate your note placements.

Exercise 5:

Ostinato 1: Ride cymbal and foot-controlled open/close hi-hat

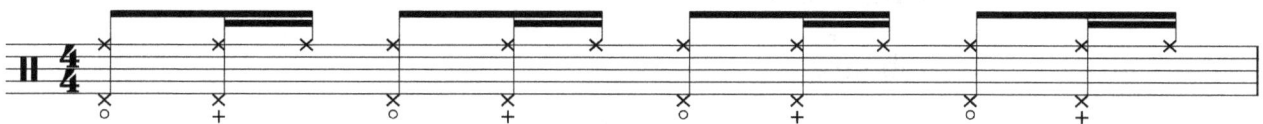

Ostinato 2: Jazz ride and hi-hat patterns

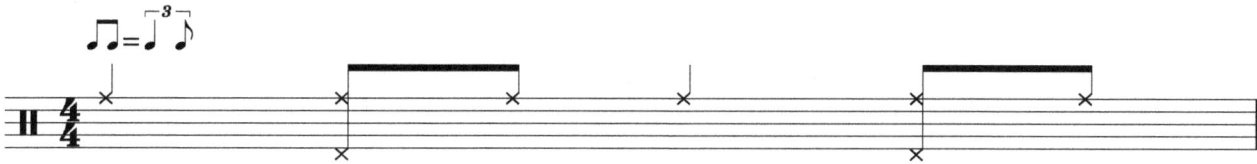

7-note grouping patterns (treat them as 8th notes when using Ostinato 2)

Session 5: Integrating odd groupings and upbeats phrasing into grooves and chops

In this session you will learn how to interpret odd groupings and upbeats. Let's work on effective sticking vocabulary, grooves, ghost notes control, and note placements.

Let's use the metronome system introduced in Session 2 from the last book:

1. Mark all 16th note subdivisions

2. Mark all 16th note upbeats

3. Mark "e"s or "a"s

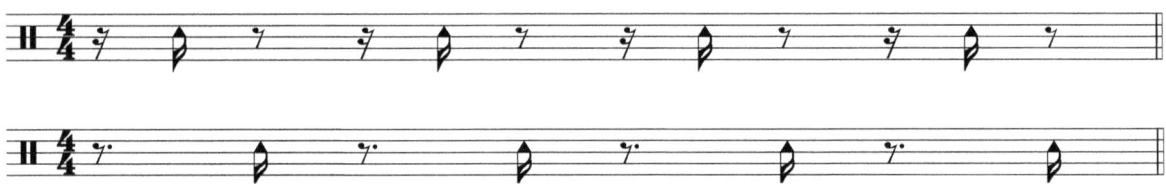

Make sure you count out loud when working on the exercises below.

For more details, please visit *"Session 2: Training on timing and note placement accuracy -- the metronome"* from my first book *"An Analytical Approach to Linear Applications: Integrating Gospel Drumming into Your Grooves and Chops"*.

5.1: From sonic vocabulary to sticking vocabulary

Please follow the instructions below and work on Exercise 1 & 2:

1. Analyze the phrases to see what groupings and upbeats elements are used.

2. Sing the melodies while clapping out the pulse with your hands.

3. Play on snare drum, and fill in the space with:

    a. Singles
    b. Doubles
    c. Paradiddles
    d. Provided example stickings
    e. Repeating **a-d** above, adding flams to the accents
    f. Orchestrating the melodies around drum set
    g. Repeating **e** above, orchestrating flams around drum set

4. Mix & match and come up with your own stickings to interpret the melodies.

Exercise 1:

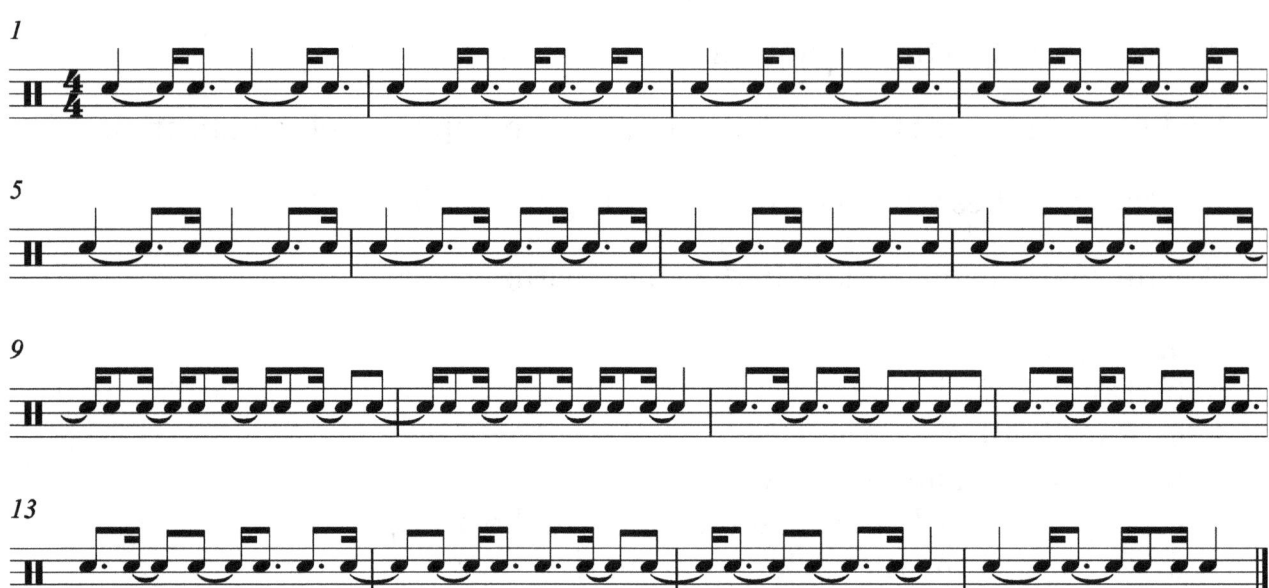

Example sticking for Exercise 1

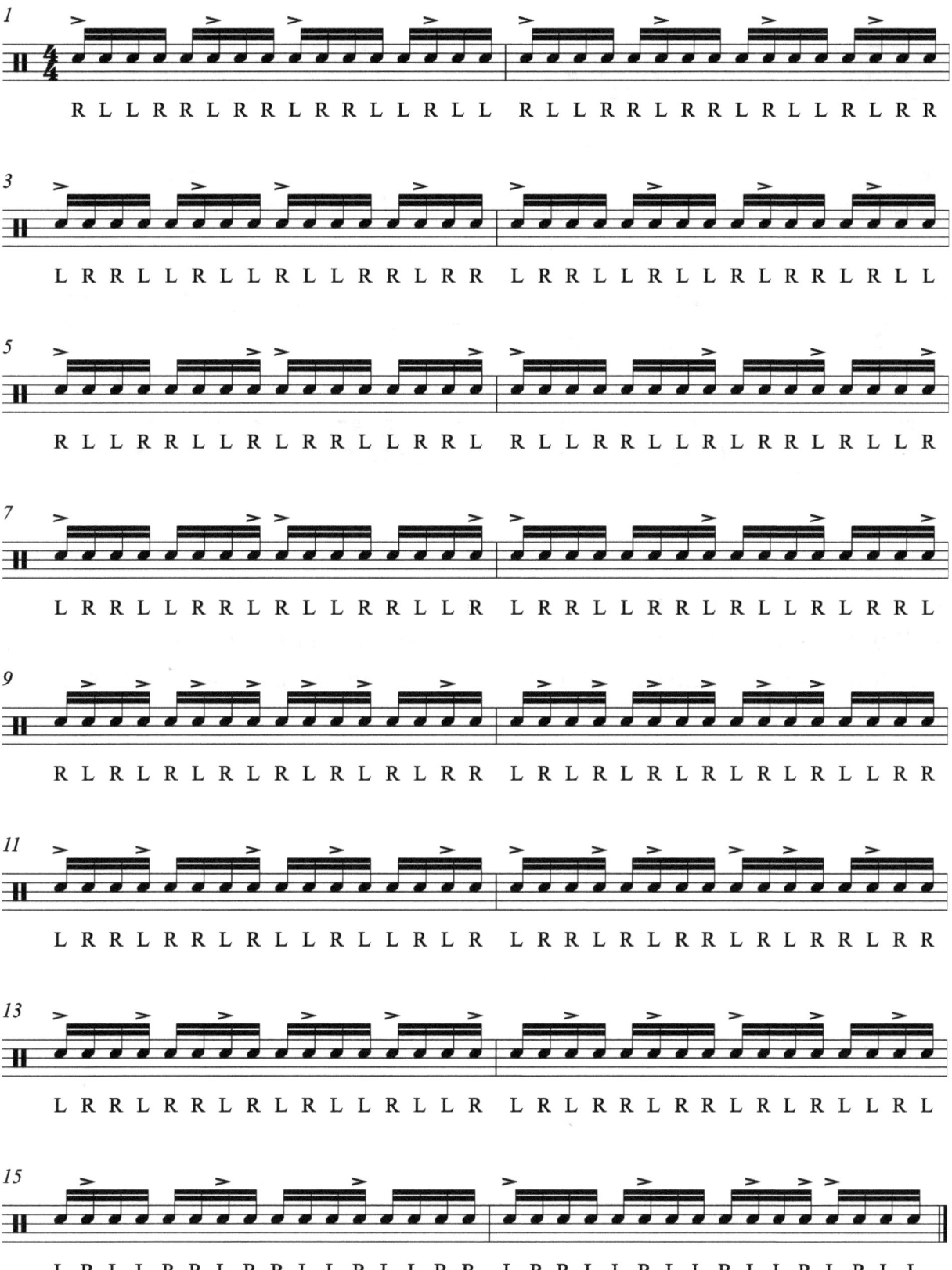

Exercise 2:

Note: In this exercise, from bar 5, you are superimposing 6/8 over 4/4. From the second half of bar 6 till the end of bar 7, the phrase is actually a 6/8 clave, you will see a 3-2 rumba clave and cascara from bar 8 to 12. Make sure not to rush the "e"s and "a"s.

Example sticking for Exercise 2

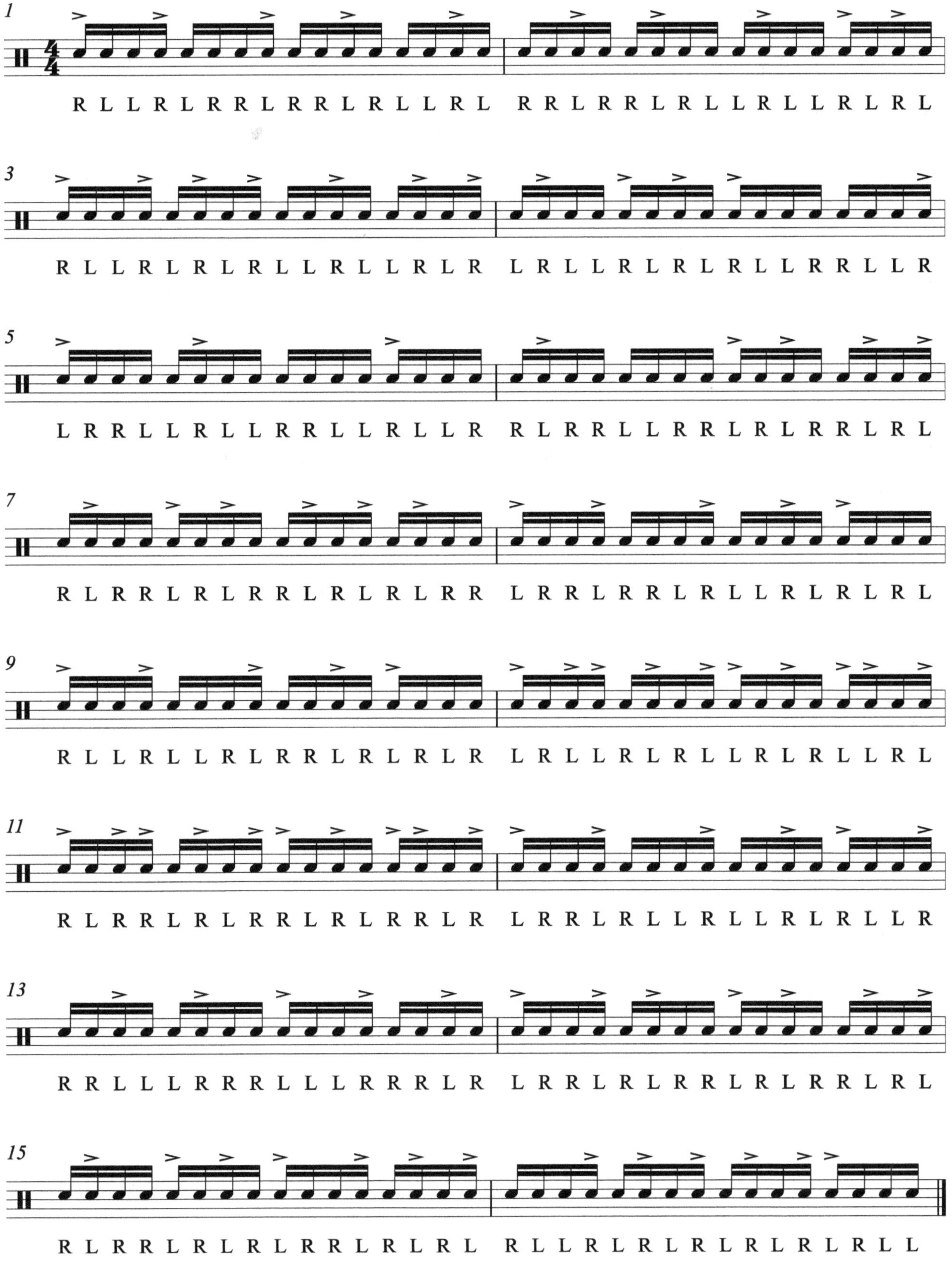

1

R L L R L R R L R L L R L R L R L L R L R L R L

3

R L L R L R L R L L R L L R L R L R L L R L R L R L L R R L L R

5

L R R L L R L L R R L L R L L R R L R R L L R R L L R R L R L

7

R L R R L R R L R L R L R L R R L R R L R R L R L L R L R L

9

R L L R L L R L R R L R L R L R L R L L R L R L L R L R L L R L

11

R L R R L R L R R L R L R L R L R R L R L L R L L R L R L L R

13

R R L L L R R R L L L R R R L R L R R L R L R R L R L R R R L

15

R L R R L R L R L R R L R L R L R L L R L R L R L R L R L L

5.2: From sonic vocabulary to groove constructions

Now let's look at two extended exercises that will help you to put odd groupings and upbeats phrasings into grooves. You will also be working on your bass drum note placements and ghost note control. Play the 32-bar melody *on the next page* with bass drum and follow the instructions in Exercise 3 & 4.

(a): Bass drum note placement

Exercise 3:

Let's bring back the ostinato from Session 3 of the first book. It can help you to align the actions of each limb accurately. For more details, please refer to *"Session 3: Bass drum placement"* in the first book *"An Analytical Approach to Linear Applications: Integrating Gospel Drumming into Your Grooves and Chops"*. Play the melodies with the bass drum under the ostinato below:

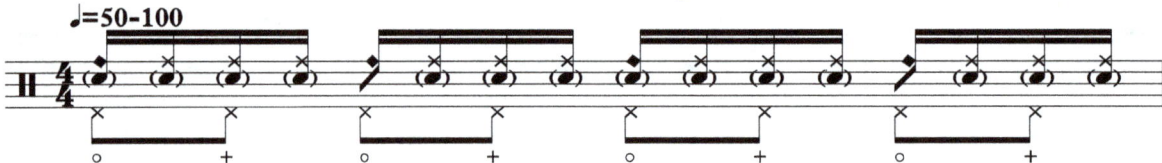

Work on the exercise in the two ways below:

1. As straight 16th note groove

2. As swung 16th note groove

(b): Ghost note control

Exercise 4:

In this exercise, let's add ghost notes to create a more *legato feel* groove. Follow the instructions below:

1. Choose an ostinato below and play pulse with your hi-hat foot

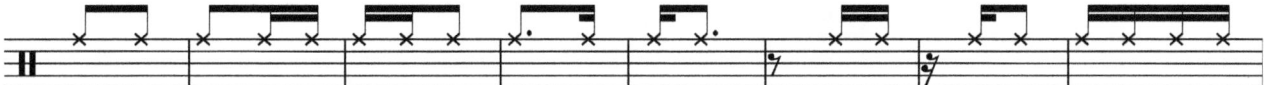

2. Choose a backbeat style from below:
   a. Regular time feel on "2" and "4"
   b. Half time feel on "3"

3. Play ghost notes on snare to fill in the blanks between bass drum melodies and snare backbeats.

4. Leave out the bass drum if a snare back beat is in place.

5. Make sure you have a clear dynamic balance between all the parts. Ghost notes should be played consistently at a lower height, and never wash off other voices.

6. Make sure you pay attention to the quality of the ghost notes. They should be consistent in rate and dynamics. Try to play them honestly with your wrists and avoid bouncing first. When you have full control, you can experiment with incorporating palming, fingers and subtle whipping motions.

7. Pay close attention to the ghost notes right before and after the backbeat and pay extra attention to micro timing stability there. There's a tendency for us to rush or drag there.

32-bar melody

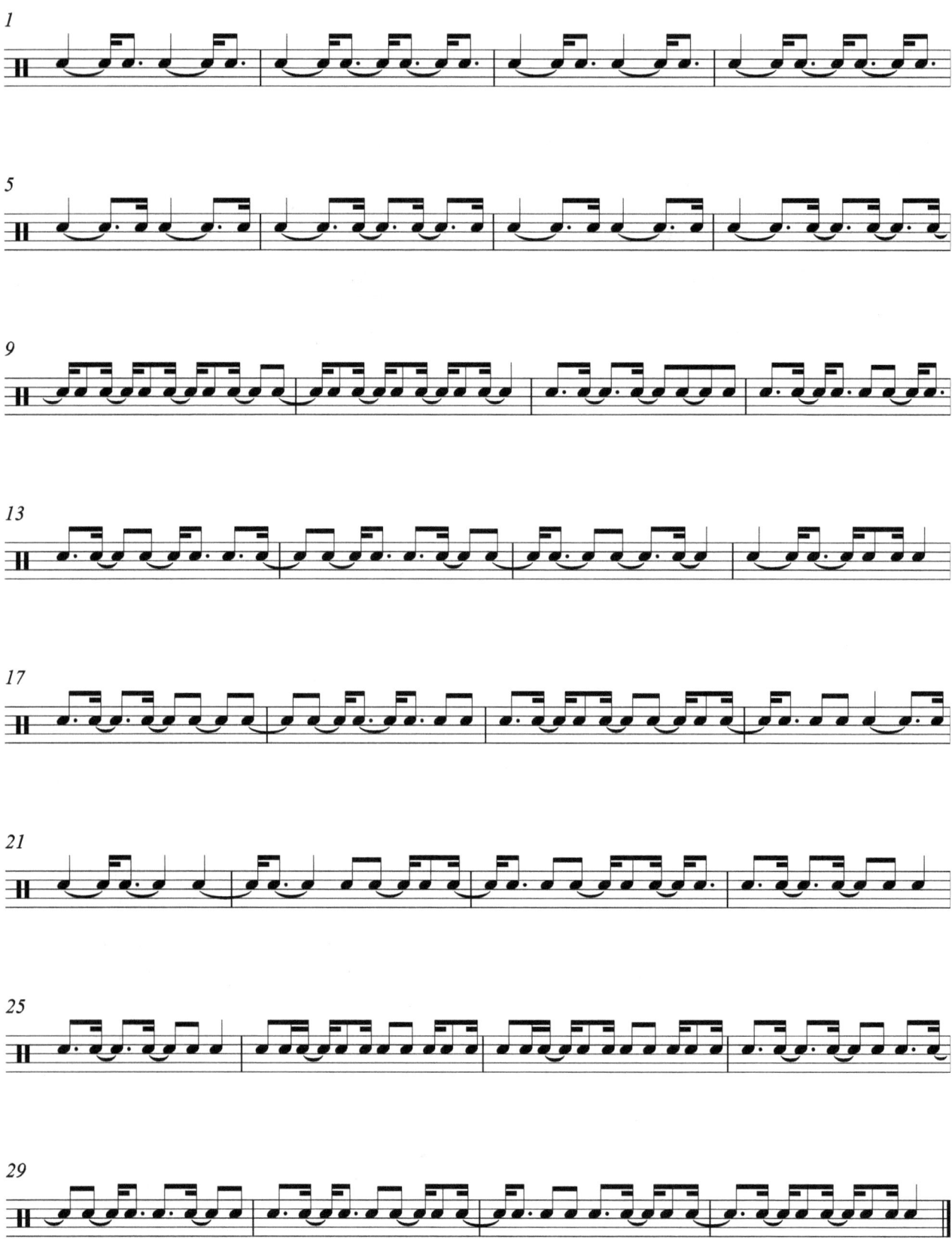

AN ANALYTICAL APPROACH TO MIND-BODY CONNECTION AND CREATIVE PHRASING

Part 2
Body:

Enhancing your mobility and *balance*

Enhancing your mobility and balance will greatly improve your flow. Part 2 of this book will provide you tools for your body to translate your mind more effectively to the drum set.

Session 6: Enhancing your mobility

Achieving better mobility on the drums will improve your efficiency and timing. In this session we will take a look at some key maneuvers around the drum set as well as irregular stickings to help you get through unexpected situations.

Let's first label each drum in the picture below.

Reference: Drum set with common configuration

1. Snare
2. Tom 1
3. Tom 2
4. Floor tom
5. Bass drum
6. Hi-hat
7. Ride

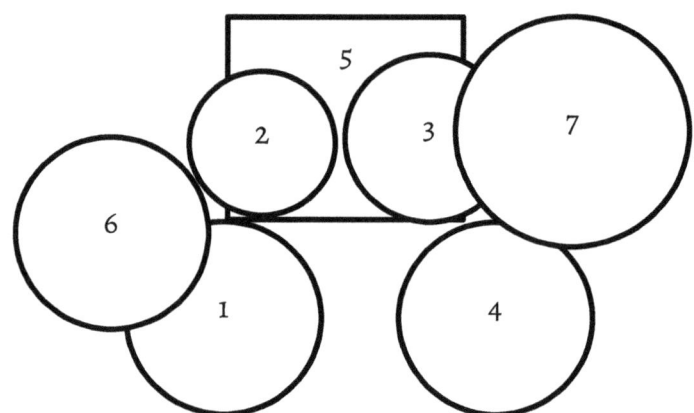

6.1: Single directional paths with single stroke roll

The single stroke roll is perhaps the most efficient way to move around the drum set. They are surely the very first thing come to people's minds when switching between drums. The most common path is to move in the order of 1, 2, 3, 4 by leading from your right hand and applying an even number of strokes (or vice versa*). When you reach the end, you will most likely land into a hit with a bass drum and cymbal to end the run, then turn around and start over again. In this way you will avoid crossovers and changing directions.

Example 1:

*To go from right to left (4, 3, 2, 1), just switch to left hand lead.

Exercise 1:

6.2: Changing directions by adding an odd number of strokes

If you want to go back and forth without crossovers in either directions, follow the guidelines below:

1. Start with the hand on the same side of your starting point. Say if you are going from left to right, then lead with your left hand from the leftmost drum.

2. Play odd numbers of strokes on the farthest drums to the left or right, or on the drums where you will change direction.

3. Play even numbers of strokes on the rest of the drums. For example, if you are moving from drum 2 to 3, you will lead with your right hand and play even numbers of strokes.

Example 2:

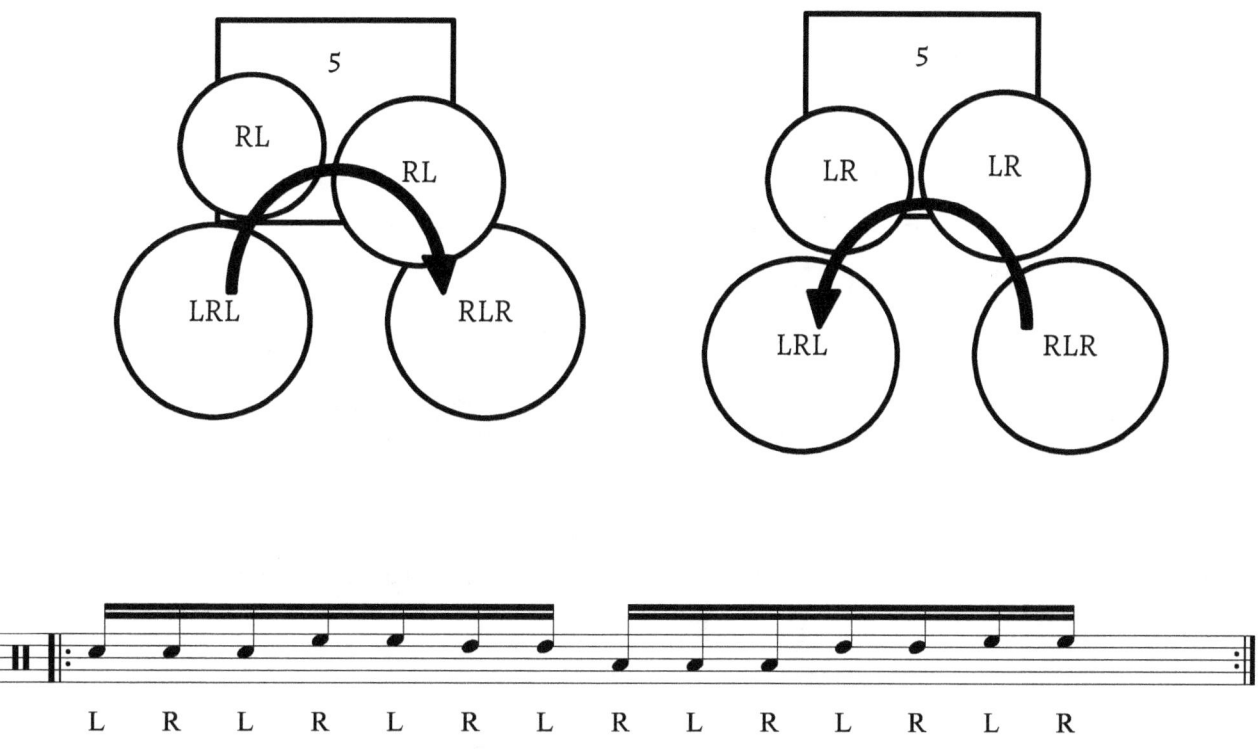

These guidelines apply to any odd or even number of strokes and any number of drums in your setup.

Exercise 2:

Apply the following alternating single stroke paths to the rate grid below. Play the quarter note pulse with your hi-hat foot. Work on each rate grid first then mix and match the rate changes.

1. |: L RL RL R LR LR :|
2. |: LRL RL RL RLR LR LR :|
3. |: LRL RLRL RLRL RLR LRLR LRLR :|

Alternating single stroke roll is probably the most agile way to change directions under any rate. It is because the relative leading hand is changing constantly per stroke. Now let's look at another way to switch directions by incorporating diddles.

6.3: Changing directions by adding diddles

Paradiddle-based sticking family also has the characteristics of changing sticking directions on a pattern basis. Even though they have a longer turn-around than an alternating single stroke roll, they still make the direction changes work great and adds some grooves to the movements.

Follow the guidelines below:

1. Start with the hand on the same side of your starting point. If you are going from left to right, then start with your left hand from the leftmost drum.

2. Play diddles, or paradiddles on the farthest drum to the left or right, or on the drums where you will change direction.

3. Play even numbers of strokes on the drums in between. For example, if you are moving from drum 2 to 3, you will lead with your right hand and play even numbers of strokes.

Example 3:

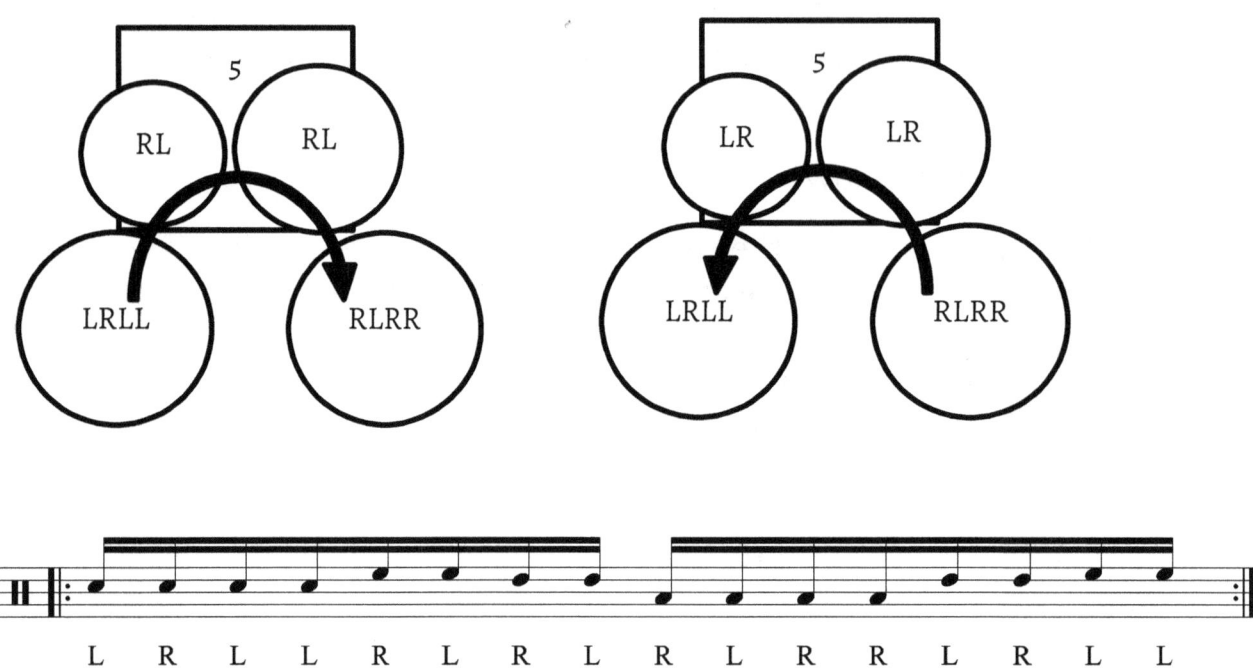

Exercise 3:

Apply the following paradiddle family paths to the rate grid below. Play the quarter note pulse with your hi-hat foot. Work on each grid first then mix and match the rate changes.

1. |: LL RL RL RR LR LR :|
2. |: LRLL RL RL RLRR LR LR :|
3. |: LRLL RLRL RLRL RLRR LRLR LRLR :|

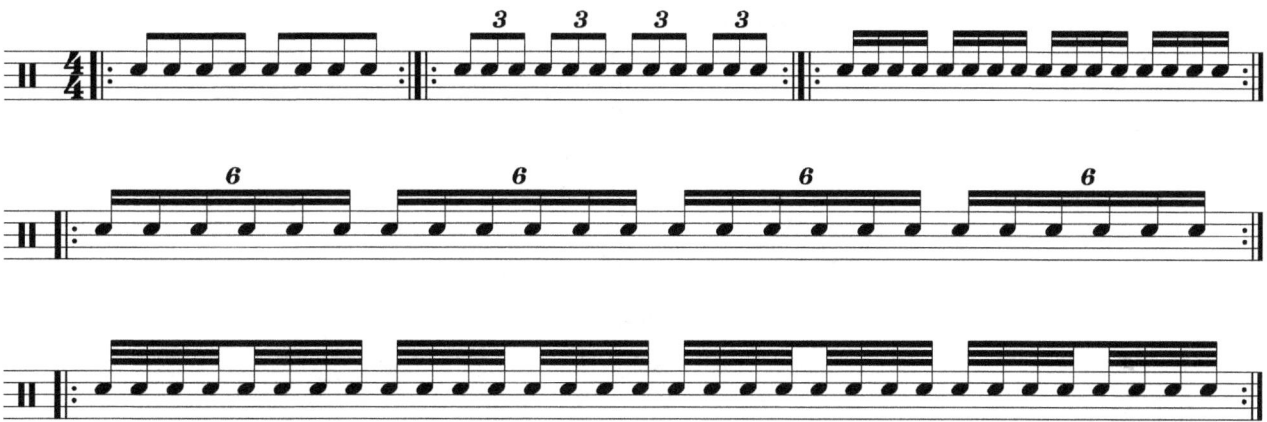

6.4: Diagnostic paths

Taking diagnostic paths between two drums back and forth could be a very effective way to improve mobility around the drum set as well. Some commonly used paths are shown below:

Example 4:

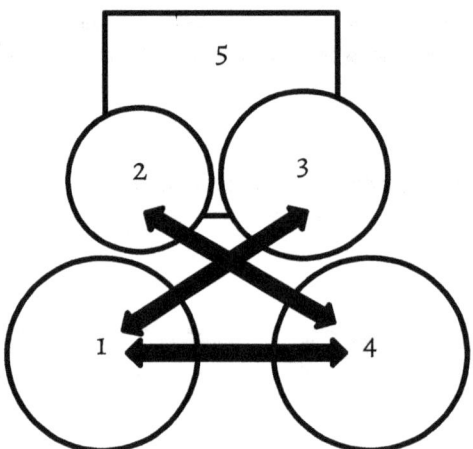

When playing with such paths, we will choose to use patterns that naturally switch leading hands, such as alternating singles, the double stroke roll, and variations of paradiddles. In the next exercise, you will be working on such paths along with some sonic patterns.

Exercise 4:

Lead with the hand on the same side of your starting point. For example, if you are starting with drums 1 or 2, then lead with your left hand. Lead with your right hand if you start with drums 3 or 4. Put everything in 4/4 now and keep the pulse with your hi-hat foot.

1. Apply alternating singles, doubles and paradiddle variations. Play 3 strokes to 6 strokes per drum. Choose a drum to start with and go back and forth to another drum. Change the starting drum and repeat. For example: if starting from 1, then you will have 1↔2, 1↔3, 1↔4. A sample path is provided for 1↔4 below.

2. Choose one or more paths and play them back to back. Apply alternating singles and doubles variations with the sonic patterns below.

6.5: Irregular stickings

Sometimes you will run into situations that your mind wants to go somewhere but your body is having difficulty keeping up. Your sticking flow would break because you are not in a familiar position to start or continue a flow. In this case you will have to move irregularly to keep the flow going. Irregular stickings are always going to be something out of your comfort zone. Let's take a look at the following couple of exercises that help your body to adapt to the unconventional movements better.

Exercise 5a:

Work on the following movements with each hand separately.

Exercise 5b:

Work on the following movements with each hand separately.

Session 7: Enhancing your balance

Balance is influencing your playing at every moment. In this session let's look at physical balances such as the balance of your position on the drum set, the balance between the dominant and weak sides of your body, the balance between your hands and feet, etc.

7.1: Balancing yourself and your drum set

You should establish a good balance between yourself and the drums every time before you play. You need to think about *(a) your posture* and *(b) the ergonomics of your drum set.*

1. Check your posture

   a. You should be seating up straight, slightly engage your core to balance your body, and relax your shoulders.

   b. Your thighs should never go lower than your knees. This will avoid adding extra tension and pressure to your knees and back. You would want to protect your knees and back as much as possible.

   c. Your ankles should not go behind your knees. This will avoid adding extra pressure to your knees when playing heel-up.

   d. A natural position would be sitting up straight and keep your neck and shoulders relaxed. Sit slightly higher than the level of your knees, and your ankles should be placed a little bit in front of your knees. Slightly engage your core to prepare for movements.

2. Check your drum set ergonomics

    a. Your drums should be placed ergonomically to assist your playing. You shouldn't work extra to reach your drums. Check your drums' spread to make sure your reaching distance is comfortable.

    b. Check your drum's height. A very natural way to figure out your drum's height is to close your eyes and pretend to play a drum in the air. Where you stop naturally should be the perfect height for you to place that drum. You could check on each drum. I learned this from Dave Weckl and it greatly improved my overall efficiency. It releases a lot of tension off my playing as well so that I don't fight with the drums anymore.

3. Memorize your seating relationships with the core components: kick, snare, and hi-hat. You can use your stick to measure the heights: for example, your seating height could be one stick plus four fingers. This will save time when you need to move and set up your drums frequently.

By checking on your posture and drum ergonomics, you can make sure that you are in the best condition before you start to play. There will be tons of other things that you need to balance in your playing, so it is very necessary for you to offload any pressure before starting to play.

7.2: Balancing your weak side

You always have your dominant side and weak side. When you play matched grips, your body's two sides will get close, but you will never feel exactly the same on both sides. So, an effective way to fix this is to try to minimize the gap between two sides, adapt to the differences at the same time, and figure out a balance to achieve a unified sonic result. This is exactly what traditional grip players can do: the two hands are using different muscle groups and different mechanisms, but they are still achieving a sonic unity.

A select group of exercises down below can help you to balance the two sides. Please be focused and feel each side clearly and know how they are different; then let the weak side copy the dominant side's motion and feel; at the same time recognize the differences and let each side find its own way to balance with each other.

Follow the instructions below for Exercises 1-3:

Work on the following exercises from slow to fast and feel the flow. If you run into any glitches, don't forget to check your posture and drum ergonomics. Work on them till you can flow naturally without tension before moving on to the new tempo.

Play on a single surface first then orchestrate the accents with *(a) toms* and *(b) cymbals and bass drum in unison*. Keep pulse with your hi-hat foot.

Add flams to the accents.

Page left blank to facilitate chart reading.

Exercise 1:

If you are left dominant, lead with your right hand.

(Continued on the next page.)

AN ANALYTICAL APPROACH TO MIND-BODY CONNECTION AND CREATIVE PHRASING

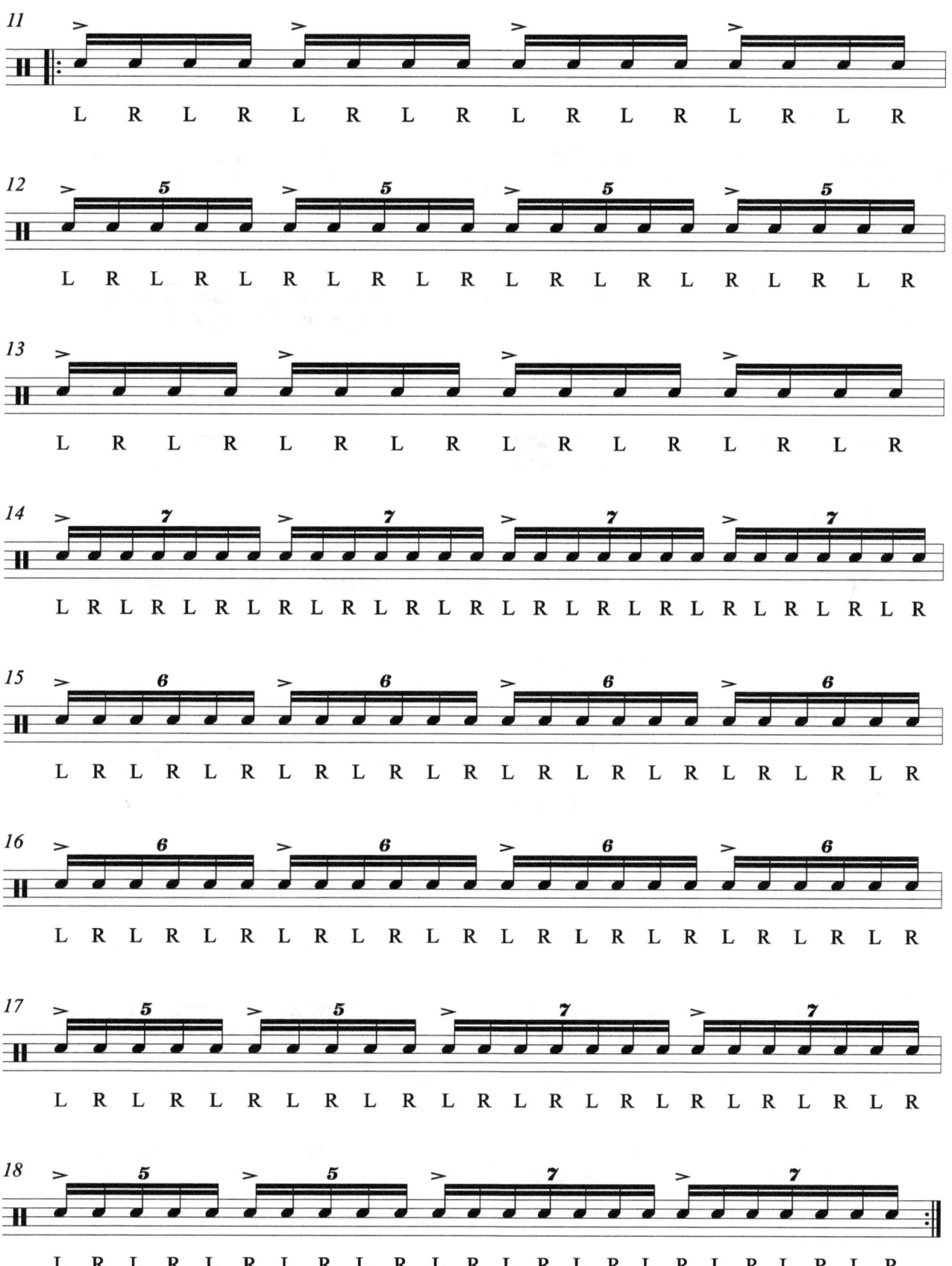

Exercise 2:

Switch leading hand at repeat.

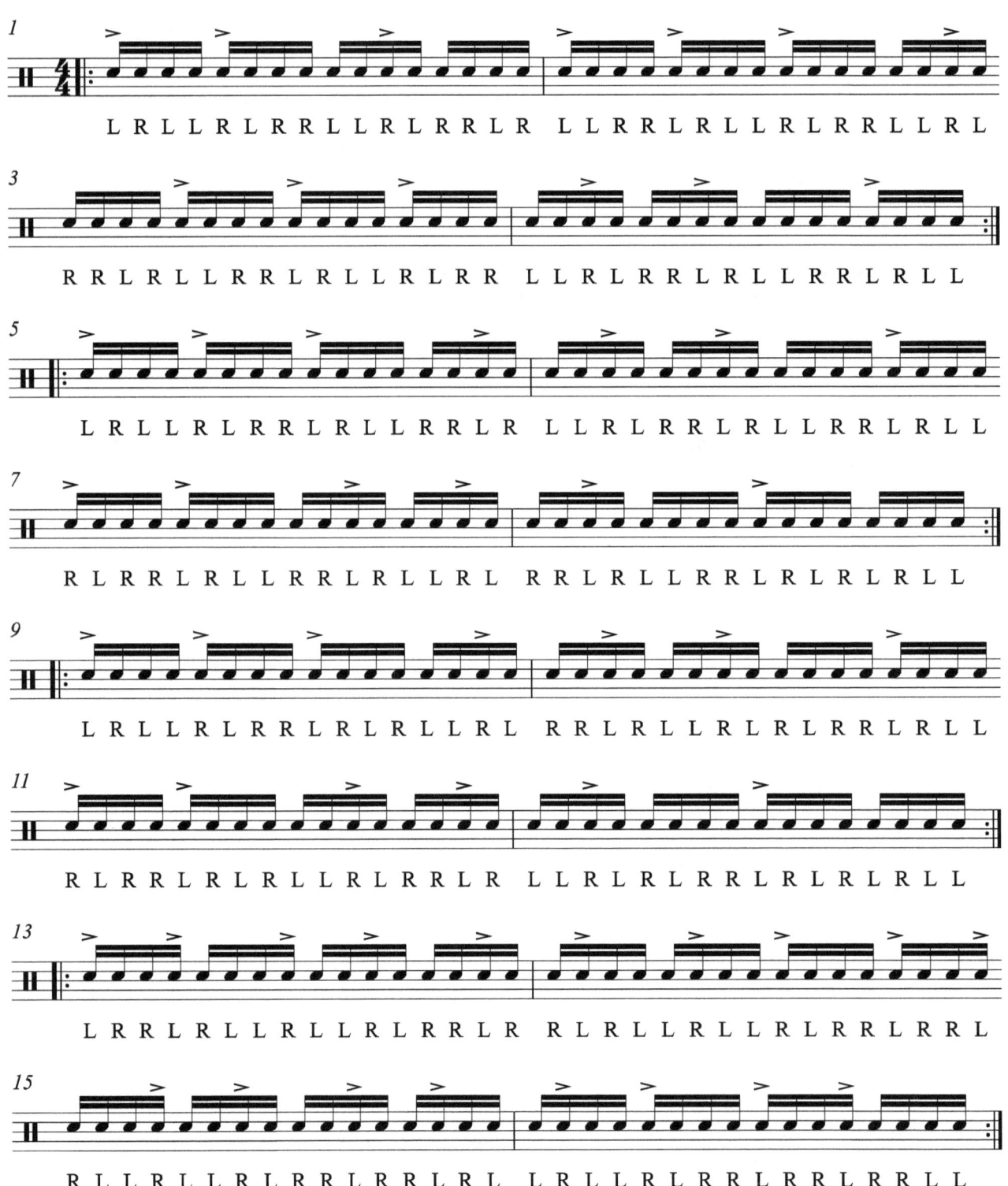

Exercise 3:

The melody below shows the accent patterns of the classic Three Camps. Play them with *(a) 8th note triplet* and *(b) 16th note*. Choose your own stickings to fill in the spaces.

For example, if you choose to use paradiddle family stickings, you could apply single paradiddles to the quarter notes and triple paradiddles to the half notes.

7.3: Balancing your hands and feet

Old-school drumming was developed more with a horizontal approach, which is to put emphasis on the relationship between both hands. Drumming nowadays is relying more on vertical linear interdependence relationship between your hands and feet. You can find in detail about linear interdependence coordination in *Sessions 6 and 7* from my first book *"An Analytical Approach to Linear Applications: Integrating Gospel Drumming into your Grooves and Chops"*. Let's move on to the following exercises to improve your vertical balance.

Exercise 4:

Work on blast beats in the given two styles below. Practicing blast beats is one of the most effective way to improve hand/foot balance. You will be playing cascara ride patterns (in 4/4 and 6/8) on top of the blast beats. These patterns are great for practicing upbeat subdivision independence.

Exercise 5:

This exercise shows the hand/foot split alternating singles Vinnie Colaiuta uses a lot: playing snare drum on the upbeats with a low volume and using bass drum and toms to create a melody. Keep a pulse with the hi-hat.

Exercise 6:

This exercise shows another hand/foot split alternating single that Dave Weckl uses a lot: play the bass drum on the upbeats and use your hands to create a melody. Keep a pulse with the hi-hat.

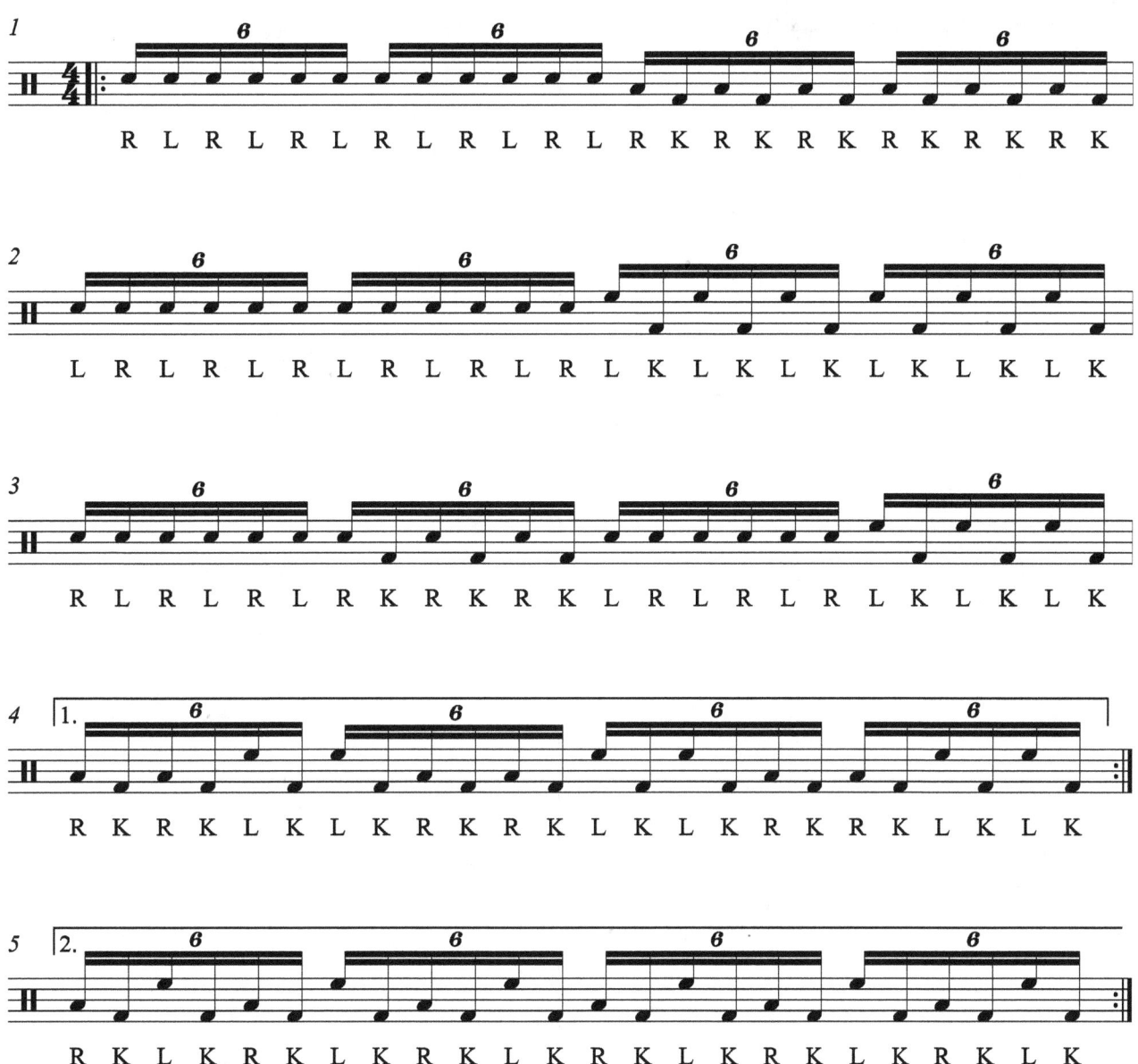

The short sprint between hand and foot requires you to adapt to the rapid switch in a very short of times. That is why these kinds of patterns are more difficult to execute. Once you are familiar with the flow, move on to the subsequent comprehensive exercises and push your limits to acquire even more advanced balance.

7.4: Advancing your balance

In this part, let's look into couple of additional exercises with more complicated switches between your hands and feet. The goal is to break up the repetition of one element and bring in new elements to improve your ability to quickly adapt to the changes. This ability will improve your physical freedom to support your phrasing later. Keep a pulse using the hi-hat.

AN ANALYTICAL APPROACH TO MIND-BODY CONNECTION AND CREATIVE PHRASING

Exercise 7:

Change leading hands at repeat.

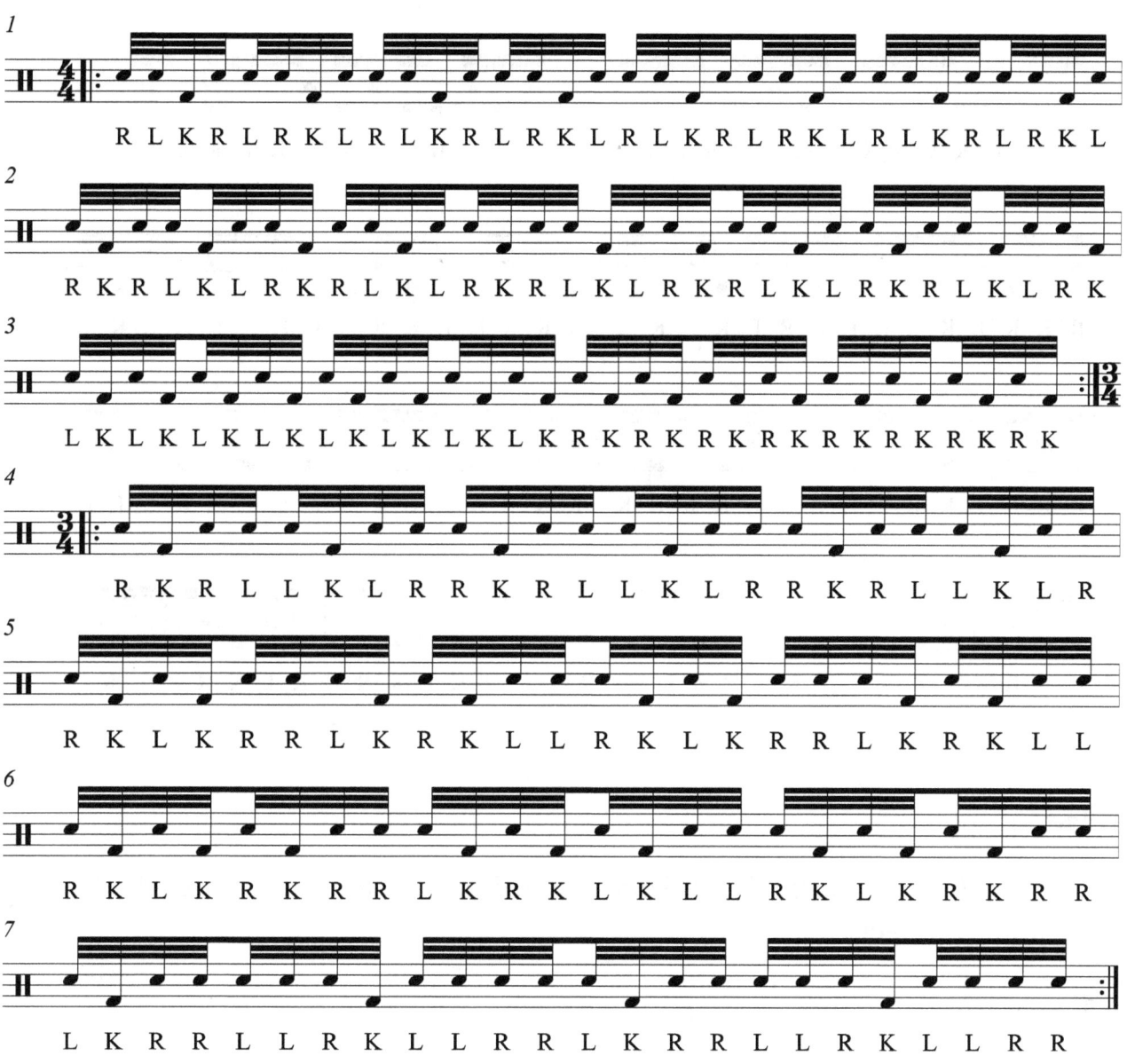

Exercise 8:

Triple paradiddle-based permutations

Exercise 9:

Work on page 6 of the classic book *Stick Control*, and assign the provided stickings to your hands and feet.

Part 3
Mind-body connection:
the Creative Phrasing *System (CPS)*

The first two parts discussed how to improve your mind and body. To train your mind, you can expand your sonic vocabulary by hearing the upbeats and odd groupings. And for your body, we looked at ways to enhance mobility and balance. With all we have talked about so far, including materials from the first book, now it's time to connect your mind and body, and start to look into creative ways of phrasing in the final part of this book.

In this part, I will discuss a series of very effective methods to improve your phrasing creativity. My great friend David Myers Jr. (Frank Ocean, 6lack, Zayn Malik) and I worked together and created the Creative Phrasing System. David's playing has always been a great inspiration to me and really makes me think differently on the approach of phrasing. We spent quite a lot of time together analyzing David's unique phrasing style and method to integrate it into my own playing to creative something new. David would then integrate my results backward into his own playing. This process went back and forth and eventually inspired us to sum up this effective series of methods.

The examples and exercises in this part are provided to help you to understand the thinking process, and eventually you should be able to come up with your own unique style.

Session 8: Exploring spaces

In this session, let's look at the first two methods in CPS: interpreting spaces at both the micro and macro levels to help with phrasing. On the micro level, let's look at the smallest elements in your phrasing process; on the macro level, let's expand the concept to larger groups of elements.

8.1: At the micro level—exploring spaces at different rates

At the micro level, let's focus on the space covered by each individual note. Let's take the quarter note figures below as a simple example. Here they represent a motif that contains four equal value figures.

Example 1:

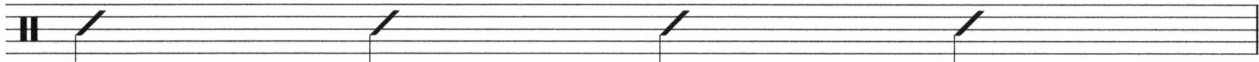

When interpreting the quarter note space, you have two choices of *(a)* playing it as it is and leaving the space open, or *(b)* giving it an emphasis on each figure and filling up the space with content in contrast. For example:

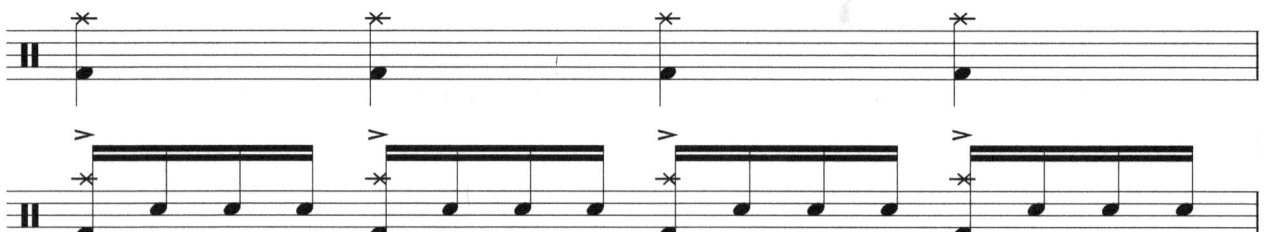

Let's take a look at the second line, which is an example of creating emphasis and contrast. With the spaces, you could freely bring in and out different rates to subdivide the figures. In this way you can create and release tension without changing the original rate structure of the motif. For example, you can use quintuplets to create more tension and then resolve it with the natural and easy 16th note subdivision.

Example 2:

In the next part, let's look at the rate changing sheet. Work on each individual of rate till quality and consistency are assured; then try to mix and match different rates.

Exercise 1:

Follow the instructions below:

1. Work on the three groups of rates marked by letters A, B, and C. Use the hi-hat to keep a pulse.

2. Apply the paths in Session 6 to each rate below.

3. Mix and match the eight different rates and work on transitions. The goal is to switch between each rate accurately and smoothly.

Exercise 2:

Play with accents first, once you feel comfortable, play without the accents.

This is a great way to keep the figures or accents in their relative positions and at the same time give the phrasing different characteristics.

8.2: At the macro level—exploring the full phrase in different ways

At the macro level, we look at the entire structure of a motif and explore it with *(a) stretch and compression of time* and *(b) relative position of figures*.

(a): Stretch and compression of time

Now let's take a look at the first effect—stretch and compression of time. In the example below, you will see a five-note motif, and a sixteen-bar AABA form melody created by keeping the same motif structure but stretching or compressing the time of each figure in the motif.

Example 3:

This is actually a very classic way of phrasing in jazz. With this method the structure of the motif remains unchanged, but by engaging *repetition, rate change* and *displacement* you get to create tension and release. The stable motif structure becomes a gravitational hearing center for listeners to easily recognize the motif and the flow of phrasing, in the meantime tension can make the music move forward. This approach is still influencing modern jazz playing significantly nowadays.

AN ANALYTICAL APPROACH TO MIND-BODY CONNECTION AND CREATIVE PHRASING

Exercise 3:

Use the following motif to create a sixteen-bar phrase. Phrase the motif using repetition, rate change, and displacement.

Now let's look at another example using time stretch and compression. This time let's incorporate odd grouping ideas from Part 1 to create a time stretch.

Example 4:

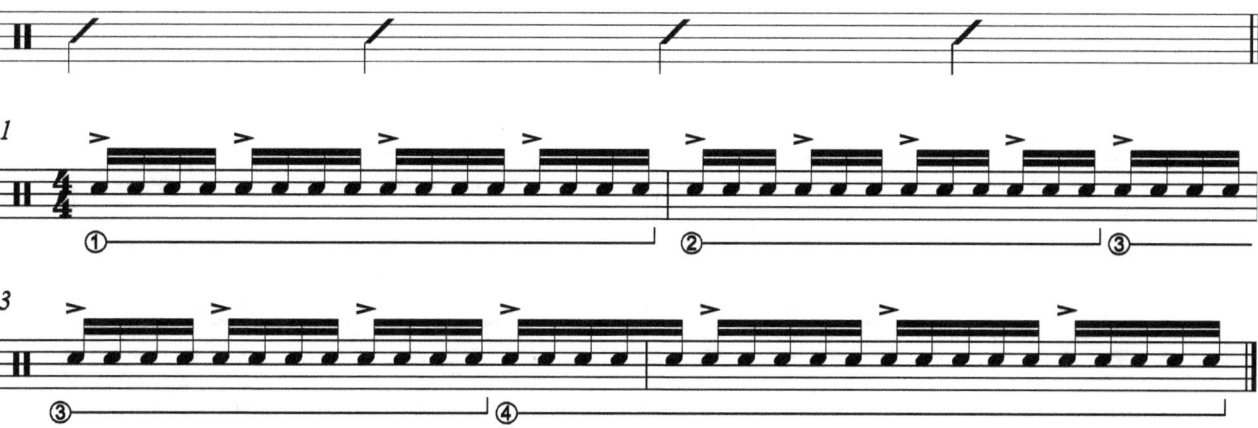

In Example 4, the phrasing idea is to fill up the spaces to connect the notes. The phrase in bracket 1 is the most straightforward interpretation of the figures. Bracket 2 contains 3-note groupings that compress the time for each figure to dotted 8th note, you will hear an accelerated 4-note motif, but it still has the same structure as the original 4-note motif—the relationship between each figure in the motif remains unchanged. In bracket 3 we are going back to the original four-note motif with quarter note values, but with a displacement of one quarter note ahead. And in bracket 4, you are experiencing a time stretch using 5-note groupings to create the same four-note motif with each figure stretched a little bit longer.

Exercise 4:

Interpret the 4-note motif above using different rates and groupings. Keep the 4-note motif cycle clear. You could mark the start of each motif by accenting with a cymbal.

(b): Relative position of figures

Let's look at the first two lines from the Exercise 2 above in 8.1. Note here how you can interpret each accent's space using different rates in bar 1 and 3, then smoothing out the rate changes using combined tuplets to create an accent pattern in bars 2 and 4 that sound similar enough to the original accent's position. This subtle change will create a smoother feel to the phrase.

Example 5:

Now let's look at the classic 5/4 rythmic pattern from "Take Five".

Example 6:

In Example 6, the first bar shows a rhythm in 5/4 with an accent pattern. In the second bar we are filling up the spaces with 8th note subdivisions. In bar three, we are applying a new rate to each accent space by dividing *(a) the dotted quarter note into four parts,* and *(b) the quarter note into three parts*, (or you can say we are engaging quadruplets and triplets for rate-changes). In bar four, we are smoothing out the rate-change by giving each new subdivision an equal value as sixteenth notes and turned it into 7/8. With a metrical tempo change to 70bpm, we are keeping the bar length the same on the time dimension and we have a new accent pattern with a very close relative accent position compared to the original ones.

This entire process is a metric modulation from 5/4 to 7/8. In Session 2, you learned the use of the pivot notes. In this example the pivot notes are the quarter notes. 5/4 and 7/8 each contains 5 and 3.5 of them. By applying the equation, you will have 100/new tempo=5/3.5, and the new tempo would be 70 bpm.

When putting bar one and five side by side, these figures should sound identical. By going back and forth you can create a stretch and compression to add different colors to your phrasing.

Exercise 5:

Work on switching back and forth between the two meters above in Example 7 in AABA form. Apply 4, 8, and 16 bar phrases into the AABA form.

Session 9: Creative sticking part 1—sticking sound texture

In the next two sessions let's focus on using sticking vocabulary to interpret the sonic vocabulary creatively. In other words, using our body (tools) to creatively interpret our mind. In this session, let's talk about the sticking sound texture.

If you pay close attention, you will find all rudiments having their own sonic textures. For example, if you are playing 16th notes evenly with singles, doubles, and paradiddles, even though they could sound very similar, you should still hear the texture differences due to the flow and motion differences. Let's look into couple of rudiments and their variations and see how you can use them to add more colors to your playing.

9.1: Sound texture of double stroke roll variations

(a): Inverted double stroke roll

Double stroke roll is versatile for connecting figures and adding a legato feel to phrases. It could also generate a very smooth flow and add a pleasant, almost fuzzy-ish sonic texture. Traditional double stroke roll is played with two strokes per hand, and the initial flow from double stroke roll is half speed of what it sounds like. In Part 1 of the book, you have worked on using upbeats and odd groupings to improve your phrasing creativity. Now let's see how you can modify the double stroke roll to add colors to your phrasing. The first example is the inverted double stroke roll.

Example 1:

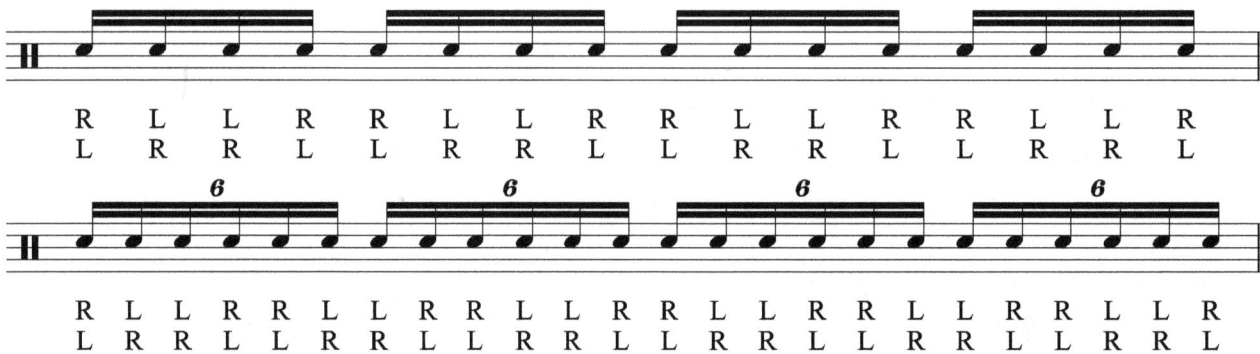

When doubles are inverted, there is a pair of alternating strokes at every downbeat. This is great because you could accent them to start a flow followed by the roll immediately afterward. This could be very useful when phrasing around a backbeat or any accent. In the next example, let's look at a 16th note-based linear syncopated half-time feel groove within a four-bar phrase. You will interpret the figures at the end of the phrase.

Example 2:

Now let's come up with a groove and see how you can use inverted doubles to interpret the figures at the end of the phrase.

Example 3:

You would hear a very legato sonic texture from the double stroke roll above. If you were to play with all single stroke roll, it could sound similar, but with a slightly more angular and articulated texture. Let's look at another way to phrase the same thing using double stroke roll in triplet rate.

Example 4:

(b): Short roll variations with similar sonic vocabulary

Now let's look at more double stroke roll variations.

Example 5:

It is not hard to tell that all patterns above share a similar basic sonic vocabulary of "dah—da dah—da", even though different rates are involved. Let's look at another variation in which the sonic pattern is displaced:

Example 6:

Coming up next is a 16-bar passage based on Vinnie Colaiuta's version of the main groove from Actual Proof by Herbie Hancock. The two sonic patterns from Example 5 and 6 above work great in this content because they can seamlessly carry over and expand the syncopated feel from the groove. Note how the phrasing below uses the two sonic patterns from the last two examples.

Example 7:

The next step is to orchestrate around the kit. Try to incorporate toms into the rolls and use cymbals to highlight the accents and figures.

Exercise 1:

Use the Actual Proof groove in Example 7 to come up with a 32-bar passage. Use the sonic vocabulary figures above in Example 5 and 6 as motifs for phrasing. This time try to orchestrate and create longer phrases. Make sure your phrases are closely related to your sonic vocabulary so that your orchestration does not sound like an exercise. Try to make it as musical as possible.

9.2: Sound texture of paradiddle family stickings

Paradiddle family stickings provide great mobility and a very distinct sonic texture. In Session 6, you learned that paradiddle family stickings usually have a natural flow that helps switching between leading hands. From the previous discussion you also know that each type of rudiment has its unique sonic texture due to the motion changes. Paradiddle family stickings contain a combination of paras—alternating singles and diddles—doubles. The "paras" have a more squared tone and "diddles" have a fuzzier pink tone. When orchestrating paradiddle family stickings around drums, you will find them very handy because of the internal motions.

You will find more about the use of paradiddle family stickings for linear groove construction in detail in my first book *"An Analytical Approach to Linear Applications: Integrating Gospel Drumming into your Grooves and Chops"*. Let's now focus on orchestrations.

Exercise 2:

Work on paradiddle family variations on the next page. Follow the instructions below:

1. Play on snare first. Pay attention to the texture differences between "paras" and "diddles".

2. Orchestrate the patterns in the following manner:

    a. Between hands and foot. For example, play all the left-hand strokes on the bass drum.

    b. Using cymbals. For example:

    c. Using toms

    all provided examples use triple paradiddles.

Summarize what sonic vocabulary could be interpreted by paradiddle family stickings.

Paradiddle family variations

These variations are also in Session 8 of my first book.

Singles (right hand lead, work on left hand lead as well)

Doubles (right hand lead, work on left hand lead as well)

Doubles Permutation: Inverted Doubles (right hand lead, work on left hand lead as well)

Sinlge Paradiddle

Single Paradiddle Permutaion 1: Inverted Sinlge Paradiddle

Single Paradiddle Permutaion 2

Single Paradiddle Permutaion 3

Double Paradiddle

Double Paradiddle Permutation 1

AN ANALYTICAL APPROACH TO MIND-BODY CONNECTION AND CREATIVE PHRASING

Double Paradiddle Permutation 2

Double Paradiddle Permutation 3

Double Paradiddle Permutation 4

Double Paradiddle Permutation 5

Paradiddle-diddle (right hand lead, make sure to work on left hand lead as well)

Paradiddle-diddle permutation 1

Paradiddle-diddle permutation 2

Paradiddle-diddle permutation 3

Paradiddle-diddle permutation 4

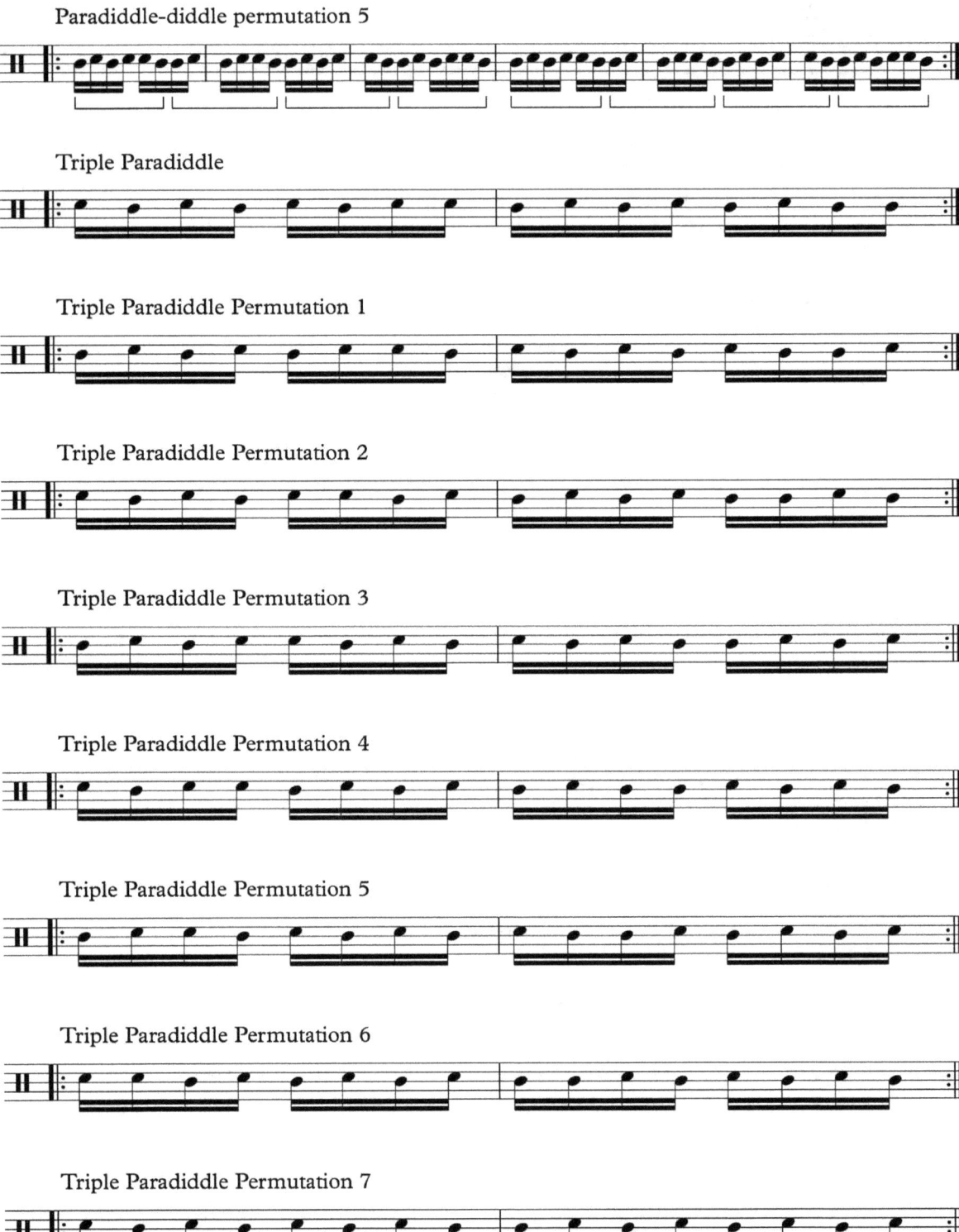

9.3: Sound texture of flams

Flams probably have the most distinctive sonic texture. They could be brighter if you play them more closed, and darker and fatter when played more open. Flams are also the perfect sonic elements to highlight a certain figure or accent. The first book provides a very detailed listing of the use of flams. Now let's review the flam variations and corresponding orchestrations.

(a): Flam variations

Example 8: Flams in alternating strokes

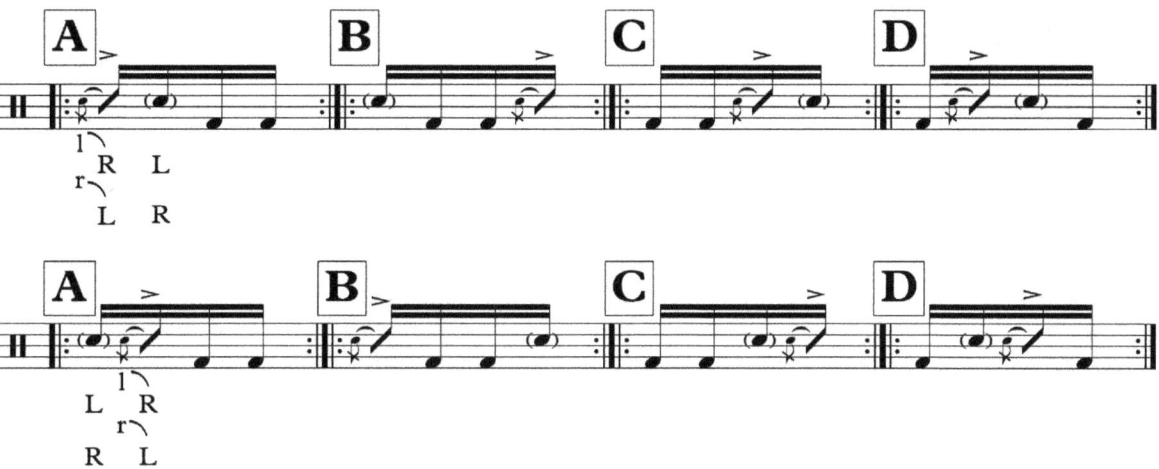

Example 9: Flams in double strokes

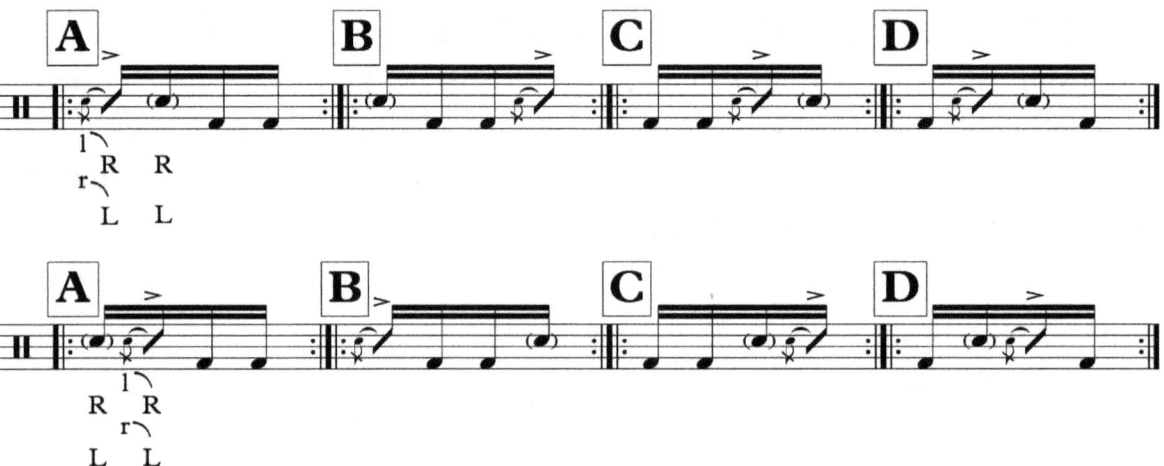

Example 10: Double Flams

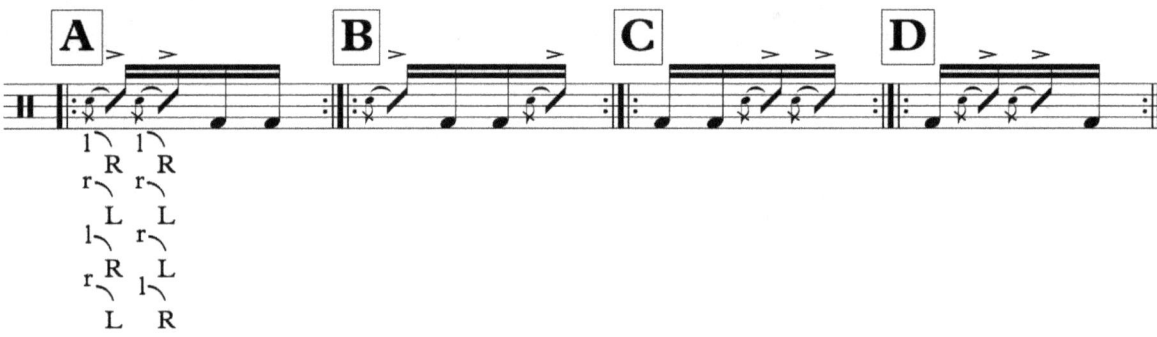

(b): Flam orchestrations

Example 11: Orchestrating variations of flam strokes

Exercise 3:

Follow the instructions below:

1. Revisit the 40 P.A.S. International Drum Rudiments flam rudiments section. Review the following flam rudiments including alternating flam, flam accent, flam tap, flamacue, flam paradiddles, single flamed mill, flam paradiddle-diddle, pataflafla, swiss army triplet, inverted flam tap, and flam drag.

2. Orchestrate the flam rudiments using the methods in the example above.

3. Know your sonic vocabulary of the flam rudiments and orchestrations, and work on transition from simple rudiments to flam rudiments. For example, if you are hearing or presented a phrase as

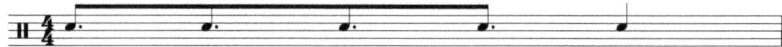

you could start to interpret it with simple stickings then move on to more advanced flams stickings.

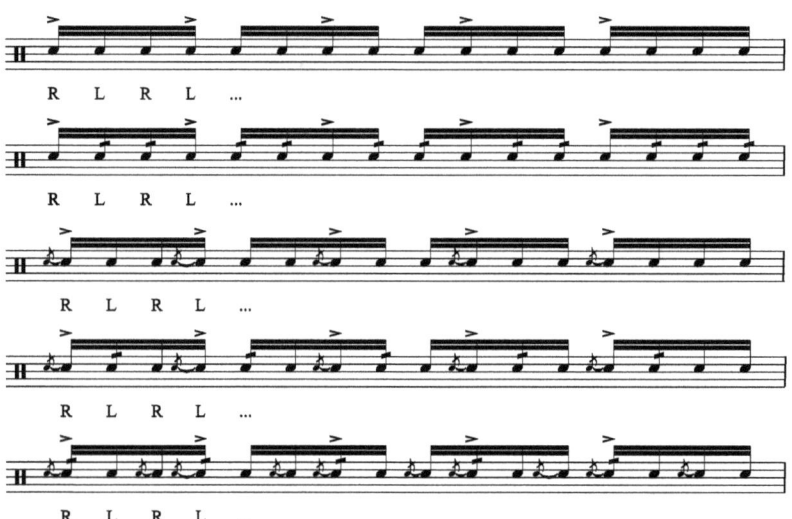

Note how these stickings all serve the same sonic vocabulary and how the sonic texture changes at each transition.

AN ANALYTICAL APPROACH TO MIND-BODY CONNECTION AND CREATIVE PHRASING

Session 10: Creative sticking part 2—sticking morphing

In the previous session, you learned about sonic textures of the three most common sticking families. In this session, let's move on and talk about sticking morphing. The idea of sticking morphing is to stretch or compress part of a sticking to morph into a different pattern with the same order of sticking. Make sure you have a good handle on the flams and drags before going into this session.

10.1: Morphing from flams

When you play flam rudiments, you have the choice to play more closed or open, depending on the tuning, musical content, and environment. For example, with a loose tuning, in a breathy and laid-back tune, or in a very reverberant environment, you probably want to play the flams more open, because open flams translate better and they could be more articulated this way. When you morph flams, you will gradually open up the flams till they flatten out. Usually it will turn into a very diddle sticking. Let's look at the example below.

Example 1:

The flam accent is a very common flam rudiment. Let's try to open the flams up and see what it could morph into. If you keep the accent at the downbeat, when you open the flam up slightly, it becomes an actual note that bounces before the downbeat.

Let's keep opening it up a bit more. Now it becomes a diddle at every third triplet.

Now you probably know that if you smooth out the humps and play each note evenly it becomes a paradiddle.

10.2: Morphing into flams

If you could morph flam accents into paradiddles by stretching the flams, then pretty obviously you could compress the same part of stickings to morph the paradiddles back into flams. Now let's take a look at the double stroke roll and see how you can morph it into alternating flams.

Example 2:

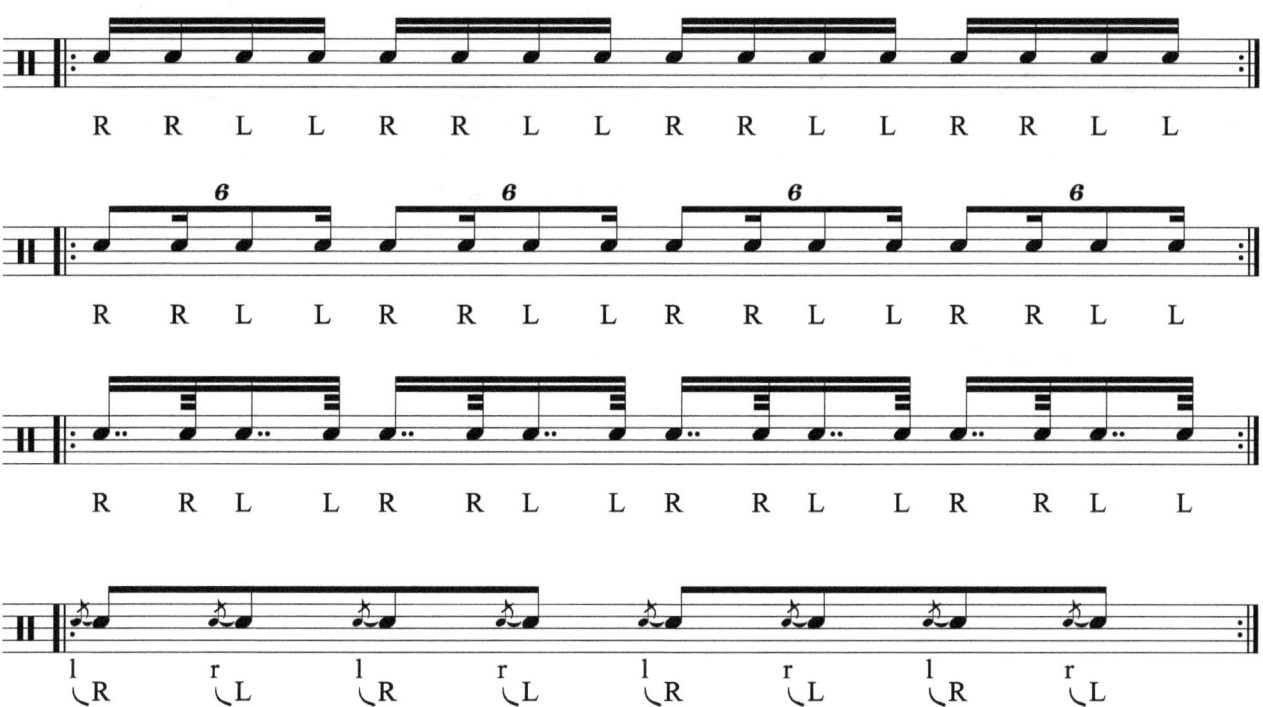

Exercise 1:

Work on the following morphing. Start from the original position in the bar on the left and gradually morph into the content in the bar on the right, then morph back to the original position gradually. Don't forget to come up with your own morphing with other rudiments and stickings.

(Continued on the next page.)

AN ANALYTICAL APPROACH TO MIND-BODY CONNECTION AND CREATIVE PHRASING

10.3: Comprehensive morphing

Now you can combine all the phrasing ideas you have learned so far. You should now have a pool of ideas to interpret a certain sonic vocabulary and morph from one to another to create the tension and release. Here is an example below. Note in bar 11, it is just easier putting the notation in 8/4; Otherwise we have to force the quintuplet across the bar line if writing in two bars of 4/4.

AN ANALYTICAL APPROACH TO MIND-BODY CONNECTION AND CREATIVE PHRASING

Example 3:

Exercise 3:

Follow the instructions below:

1. Build up a groove:

    Play four-bar phrases in 4/4 with backbeats on "2" and "4". Create a bass drum melody for the first two bars and phrase the melody around the drum set using the ideas we talked about so far in this session. If you choose to play a busy and syncopated melody on bass drum, that's fine too; just simplify to the key figures and phrase around the drum set. Again, here you are trying to get familiar with interpreting similar sonic vocabulary in different ways.

2. Develop a solo:

    Start with a motif and develop a solo using all you have learned so far about the CPS. You may gravitate to a structure first, such as the traditional AABA form, then repeat it and open it up with different interpretations. You could always write down a road map of how your motif flows through the form, and even include your detailed interpretations. When you get more familiar with your form and sonic vocabulary, you can start to phrase spontaneously without breaking the flow. Don't forget to keep working on Part 2 of the book to gain more physical freedom over the drum set.

Session 11: Displacement and metric modulation

We have briefly touched base on displacement and metric modulation in the previous sessions. They create different time and space illusions to your phrasing and create tension, making music going forward. In this last session explaining the CPS, let's look into displacement more in detail to gain freedom and creativity for your phrasing.

11.1: Permutation

In tonal music, when you permutate a scale you will get different modes. Each mode will have its own key center and related chords. Let's perceive rhythms in the same manner. When you permutate a pattern, you gain a different sonic flow on top of the same physical flow. It will inspire your creativity significantly if you absorb the new sonic flows and still be able to feel the same physical movements. Working on permutations of a certain pattern will help you improve the sense on every subdivision, especially the upbeats, as well as breaking your habit patterns that repeat unconsciously.

Example 1:

Example 1 shows the very common six stroke roll pattern and its five permutations. Note how the permutation shifts the accents through every possible variation. Your physical flow will still be the same RLLRRL or LRRLLR, but mentally you will have to do some work. You should be able to hear each permutation as a new pattern, as well as displaced.

LANG ZHAO

Exercise 1:

Follow the instructions below and work on the exercise:

1. Work on each variation and get familiar with the flow. Keep in mind the feel of the same physical flow in each variation.

2. Play time for four bars and play the permutation for four bars

3. The permutation grid below is created by shifting each permutation a 16th note behind. Play each bar continuously, by omitting the last note of each bar to connect them seamlessly (last note in each bar is the same as the first note in next bar). This will result in each bar becoming 15/16.

Cascara-based groove permutation grid

At this point you could try to come up with your own rudiments or groove permutation exercises, especially for those habit patterns that you have been repeating unconsciously.

11.2: Phrase displacement/short turn-around patterns

You could always try adding in a short turn-around pattern to keep the ideas flow. It could be as simple as one extra note on bass drum, or couple of notes on snare. This short turn-around pattern will displace your idea naturally. Let's look at exercises below.

Exercise 2:

Work on the paradiddle shift while keeping a quarter note pulse on bass drum. Feel the displacement flow mentally and physically.

Note that the bar of 3/16 is the turn-around bar. Try to lead with your left hand as well.

AN ANALYTICAL APPROACH TO MIND-BODY CONNECTION AND CREATIVE PHRASING

Exercise 3:

Work on the following patterns. Play four bars of grooves followed by four bars of the patterns. Displace them by putting in one extra bass drum note at every four repeats of the patterns. Orchestrate the patterns around the kit.

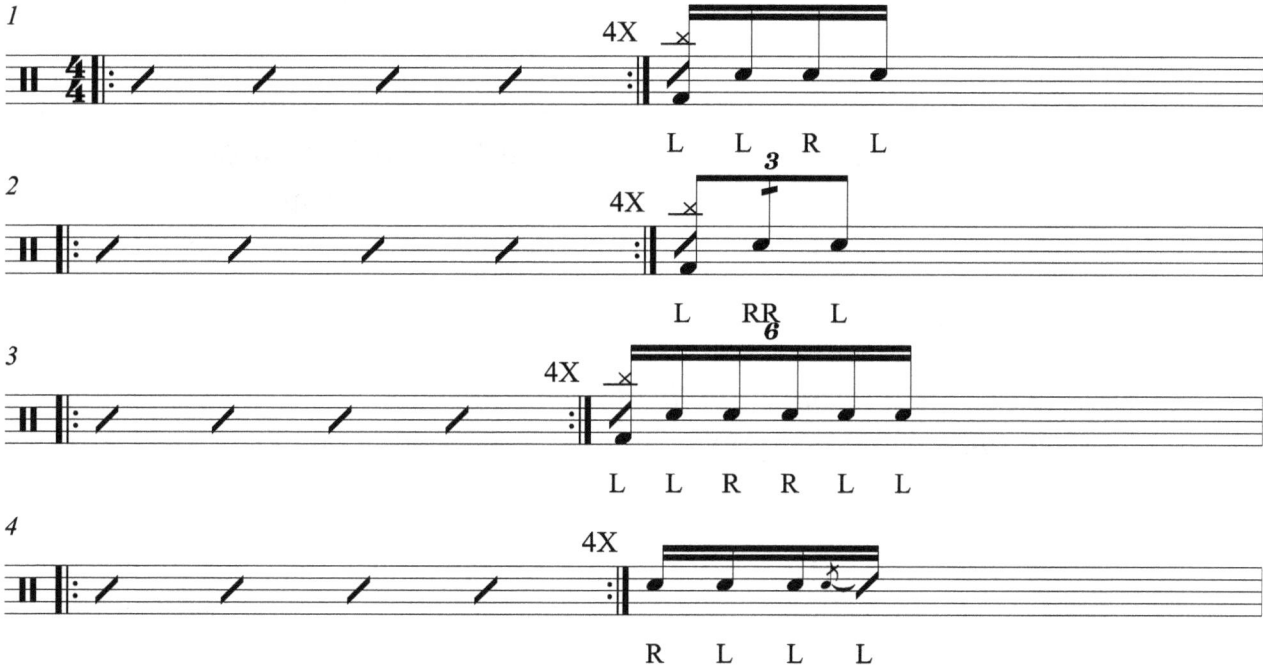

These exercises with the instruction should be able to give you a good idea so far. Try out your own playing with any stickings and sonic vocabulary.

11.3: Metric modulation

In Session 2, 3, and 8 we have talked about the concept of metric modulation and a couple of its variations. Review the sections if needed for details. Metric modulation could create a lot of tension and colors for your phrasing as long as you know where you are at and know your resolution. Let's analyze two real world examples in next session.

Session 12: Real world example analysis

In this session let's analyze two solo excerpts from my most recent progressive metal album *The Resonance Project (2019)* and see how the Creative Phrasing System is used in the music.

In 2018, I teamed up with my longtime good friend Yas Nomura and started our duo project *The Resonance Project*. This album is created in the form of progressive metal, by merging improvisation and different music elements such as jazz, fusion, gospel, orchestral music, etc. to create a refreshing listening experience.

To listen to the full songs and drum solo excerpts, please visit:
http://www.langzhaomusic.com/book-a2

12.1: Drum solo excerpt 1 analysis—The Resonance Project "Neo Thangka"

See rhythmic chart below the analysis. Letter A starts from 00:23 in the video.

Neo Thangka is one of my compositions off the album that is heavily inspired by the genre of neo jazz. Thangka is a Tibetan Buddhist painting with very vibrant colors. This song has a similar spectrum scope, so our band manager named the tune Neo Thangka.

This drum solo was improvised in studio based on a very rough sketch of the energy flow. You will see how I incorporated all the Creative Phrasing System concepts discussed in this book. All the decisions I made were spontaneous reactions to the energy and sonic vocabulary I had in mind at those moments.

The drum solo comes right after Yas and our guest artist Mateus Asato's guitar trading. It is a 32-bar solo in 3/4. The guitar trading had already built the energy up to a certain level, and I needed to start from there to build up even more to reach the climax of the song. In other words, I didn't really have too much headroom for the volume. In this case I had to structure my solo depending on phrasing to build the solo up by creating tension and releases.

Letter A shows the first 8 bars of the solo. I started with keeping the same 16th note momentum from the guitar trading in 3/4. By omitting the backbeats and phrasing around the upbeats, I was creating a more syncopated theme as an opening statement of the solo. Here I was keeping the theme simple by using ride cymbal, bass drum, and snare only. In bar 3, I created a little bit more tension by bringing in odd groupings and a new sonic pattern influenced by the iconic Tony Williams phrase in five. In bar 4, I was keeping the same sonic concept but reinterpreting the space with a rate change from 16th notes to 12th notes to create a feel of dramatic speed drop. This rhythmic distortion pushed up the tension, then the entire phrase had a release going back to the 16th note rate flow at the end of letter A. The continuous emphasis on the "e"s and "a"s in this part was also setting up the metric modulation and displacement in letter B.

Letter B started with a metric modulated groove with one 16th note displacement in bar 9, 10, and 11, bringing the energy level one step up. In bar 12, I started to resolve this a little bit by reversing the full process. I went back to the normal 16th note feel by re-emphasizing the "e"s and "a"s in bar 12 and the 5-note grouping sonic vocabulary elements from letter A. I also re-orchestrated them with flams to add more intensity.

Letter C's energy kept going up. I used a 32nd note rate phrase that kind of has that Mark Guiliana vibe to push the intensity up. From bar 18, I changed the rate again by bringing in the 12th note pulse. With a re-grouping of every 4 notes, I created a strong statement with massive tension. You could hear the classic Vinnie Colaiuta inspired flammed rolls pushing the intensity to a new level.

In the second half of letter C, I started to set up for Letter D, which is the climax of the song. I used metric modulation again, and completely changed the flow from 3/4 to 4/4 using 4:3 as the new pulse.

Letter D is the climax. Here I played a big section of gospel chops in the new modulated 16th note rate to keep pushing the energy up. The space was reinterpreted by a 42:4 tuplet, which was broken down into two bars of 19+23, to hit the climax. Then I hit that 1 in bar 33 and released all the tension.

AN ANALYTICAL APPROACH TO MIND-BODY CONNECTION AND CREATIVE PHRASING

Neo Thangka drum solo excerpt rhythmic chart

12.2: Drum solo excerpt 2 analysis—The Resonance Project "A Progression to Infinity"

See rhythmic chart after the analysis. Letter A starts at 00:03 in the video.

A Progression to Infinity combines prog metal rhythms, jazz harmony, and modern cinematic hybrid scoring. The drum solo comes after an intense half-time feel chug. Then after the drum solo, it comes the climax of the tune—the repeat of theme melody. The entire drum solo is in 15/16.

While Neo Thangka's drum solo was improvised spontaneously, the drum solo from A Progression to Infinity was pre-written. Why? First of all, it is a metal solo that has even less headroom for the energy to build up, and I needed to make it as brutal as possible but still musical and expressive. Secondly, I have to admit that 15/16 was completely out of my comfort zone back when I was preparing for the recording session. I was lucky to have my great friend and mentor Matt Garstka sharing some of his experiences and that greatly inspired me to create this solo.

The parts before letter A is the half-time feel chug. It came right after the regular time feel chug. In order to create a smooth transition from 4/4 to 15/16, I modulated the entire chug by forcing it into a 15-note grouping phrase. You could see bracket 1 and 2 are the exact same phrase but superimposed into different groupings and meters.

I started the solo from a groove-based motif, which is the 8 bars of letter A. I divided 15/16 into three 5/16 groups with backbeats, and got a "3" feel groove. To build up the energy in letter B, I created a polyrhythm by dividing 15/16 into five 3/16 groupings and let it go simultaneously on top of the original 5/16 groups. The accent patterns of both 3-note and 5-note groupings created this new rhythmic melody. Based on that melody, I created the letter B groove. You go to Session 3 to see how this polyrhythm works in detail. By shifting rhythmic structures, I created tension to motivate the flow.

The solo came to its second half in letter C. I needed to bring the energy to a higher level, so I chose to play all the subdivisions and more cymbals to intensify the flow. I was also phrasing around the upbeats and using different groupings to create more rhythmic distortion for tension. In order to lead to letter D where the energy was peaking in the drum solo, I interpreted the spaces by changing the rate from 16th note quintuplets to 32nd notes.

In letter D, I hit it strong with a call and response between snare and double bass using hertas to emphasize the downbeats. From the second half of letter D, I started using a massive amount of 32nd notes chops with double bass to fully boost the energy. It then resolved to three groups of 5/16, which I orchestrated with unison tom hits to prepare for the climax.

A Progression to Infinity drum solo excerpt rhythmic chart

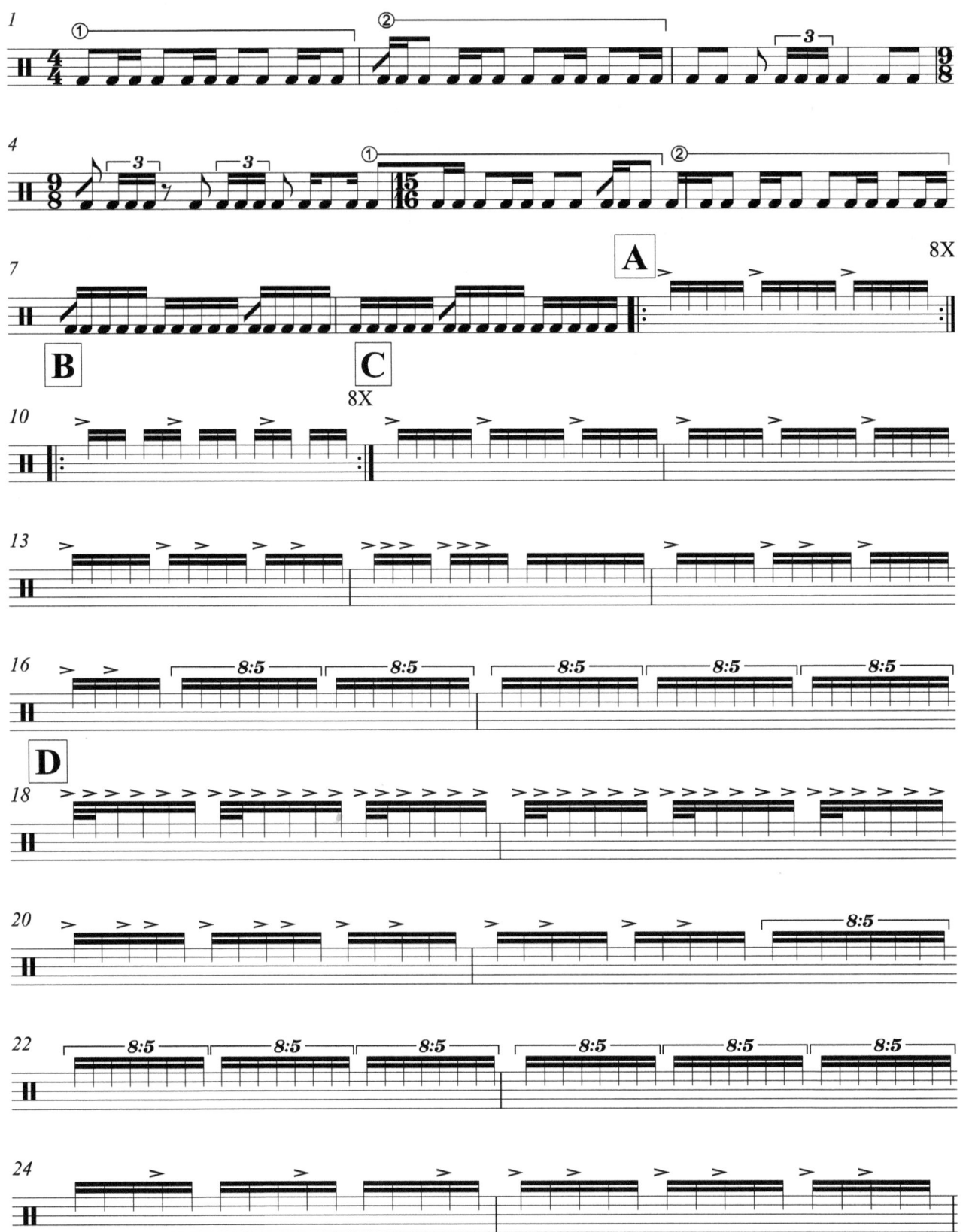

Conclusion

In the end, the goal is to find our own voice and create the best music we can create. Strong mind, body, and mind-body connection will help us phrase our ideas creatively. The drum set is not only a rhythmic instrument, but also a melodic instrument; it is just more abstract that it requires us more efforts to achieve great musicality. But abstraction also provides us with unlimited imagination.

Here comes the end of our journey of the second book from the series.

ABOUT THE AUTHOR

Lang started to study piano at the age of 4 and orchestral percussion at 14. A classical training brought him solid and effective foundational approaches to learning different instruments and music.

Before coming to the U.S., Lang was a multi-award winner both on piano and drums in China.

After graduating from Ohio State University, Lang moved to L.A. to attend Musicians Institute to further study drums. Here he received the 2013 Musicians Institute Outstanding Player Award. He was also featured at DrumChannel Live around that same time.

Lang went on to become a staff member at Musicians Institute afterwards. He stayed in L.A. to further research the art form of drumming and to study with/ receive mentorship from the drumming greats such as Rob Carson, Chuck Silverman, Matt Garstka, Mark Guiliana, Will Kennedy and many others.

In 2017, Lang published his first book *An analytical approach to linear Applications: Integrating gospel drumming into your grooves and chops*, with demonstration by Henry McDaniel IV (Big Sean, George Duke/Stanley Clarke band). It hit #1 in Amazon`s Music Technique Book category within 24 hours of its release.

Following with the book`s success in the US, the Chinese version was published in China in 2018 and became one of the most talked-about drumming books there. In the same year, Lang went on a clinic tour in China, and shared his knowledge and experiences with hundreds of drummers and students.

In 2019, Lang partnered with guitarist/bassist Yas Nomura and released their debut progressive metal album as The Resonance Project. This self-titled album is "mostly a rich jazz-fusion inflected take on modern progressive metal" (Prog Magazine, issue 99). With his rich knowledge in different music genres, and talents of composing, orchestrating, and playing, Lang created an otherworldly music vision in the album.

Later, Lang was invited by Vic Firth and played a tune from the album with Yas in a vfJams video.

The advantages from Lang`s diverse cultural background and past experiences not only allowed him to become a versatile drummer, but also offered him very effective and efficient approaches to analyze and summarize information systematically from a very unique point of view.

Lang currently works as a drummer and composer. He is also working on a series of books on drumming that cover a variety of topics that range from playing technique to different styles, including research on gospel influenced drumming.

www.ingramcontent.com/pod-product-compliance
Lightning Source LLC
Chambersburg PA
CBHW062132160426
43191CB00013B/2271